Islam 101

Ultimate Guide to Understanding Islam

Javed Mohammed

Foreword by: Hamza Yusuf

CONNECTIONS

Milpitas, CA
USA

Library of Congress Preassigned
Catalog Card No. :2002093893
Revision 1.1

ISBN 0-9701261-1-5

Printed in the United States of America

Acknowledgements

A ll praise is due to God and peace on his Prophet, who allows all societies to function through great people. There is a famous saying," I have drunk from wells I did not dig; I have been warmed by fires I did not build; I have been shaded by trees I did not plant." In similar light, Islam101 and I have benefited from writings I did not write, sayings that I did not collect, editing from those who have knowledge that I do not possess, and graphics from imaginations that are not mine.

I am indebted to all the writers whose work has allowed this book to come to fruition and the following: Omar Ahmad, Chairman of Council on American Relations (CAIR) and Razi Mohiudin, for holding a series of Open Houses after September 11th. These outreach events helped me recognize the need for this book. Dr. Muzamil Siddiqui and Dr. Abdalla Idris, former presidents of Islamic Society of North America (ISNA), checked the manuscript for errors, from an Islamic perspective.

Dr. Gerald Grudzen, Chiara DeGeronimo, Amina Jandali, Narjes Misherghi, Claire Warren, Dr. Irfan Sadaat, Dian Alyan, Shaista Azad, Sally Habbak, Sarah Azad, Jana Agbdelgawad, Nasir Mohammed, Roy and Diane Gordon who did the editing, and Imam Hamza Yusuf for the Foreword. Finally, no book is complete without the cover by Kaneshka Salehi; the layout by Banafsheh Sheikholeslami and the graphics by Omar Ali and Irfan Rydhan. May God give all those who contributed the best of rewards.

I thank God for being blessed with a great family, including parents whose prayers have built my foundations. To my teachers, wife, children, sisters, relatives and friends: may you all receive everlasting rewards for your help and encouragement.

Foreword

During this time of confusion concerning the religions of humanity in general and Islam in particular, it is important for thinking people everywhere to understand the central beliefs of other people. A belief, unlike an opinion cannot be convincingly proven false, hence the endurance of religious faith among humanity.

Beliefs may indeed be false in ultimate reality but it has what the philosopher Karl Popper would call an "unfalsifiable element," which so clearly distinguishes it from science, which is probably sciences central appeal to modern man. However, science for all intents and purposes will not provide people with nourishing beliefs that make their lives more meaningful and answer for them questions not of how but of why, not of fleeting concern but of ultimate concern. Religion while performing these tasks so well can not be proven true or false, right or wrong. Some may make more "sense' than others, but since when did sense and reason ever have anything to do with why people believe what they do? The majority of humanity are not scientists in fact very few are and ever have been. On the other hand, Science not only can but must be open to falsifiable tests before it is accepted as fact.

Religion is not science and any attempts to make it so are ultimately foolish and self-defeating. Religion and science in the West have had a tenuous relationship and open displays of hostility from both camps are still prevalent in the West. Islam has been fortunate in having a more irenic time with science, although the criticisms are there from both camps also. It is hoped that the Western world will set aside many of the prejudices toward religion as a result of her increasing infatuation with science for the last five hundred years. Also that it reassess religion in general and its central importance in the life of man and Islam in particular, given that so many people around the globe adhere to it as their faith.

This small and concise book is an excellent attempt at trying to bridge the widening gap between Muslims and others and helping people understand a profound yet deceptively simple faith, whose inner depth and complexity have for centuries engaged some of the greatest minds of humanity and inspired countless works of theology, law, science and art. Islam is still spreading and new converts emerging in the West indicate it speaks pertinently and powerfully to modern and postmodern people.

Hamza Yusuf
(Imam and Director Zaytuna Institute)

In the Name of God, the Compassionate, the Merciful

Dedicated to

This book and prayer are dedicated to seekers of truth and justice.

"O people! We created you from a single pair of a male and female, and made you into nations and tribes, so that you may know each other. Indeed, the most honorable amongst you in the sight of God is the most righteous

TABLE OF CONTENTS

Preface

Each time we as humans experience a disaster, natural or man made, its magnitude always seems to exceed that of what came before. For me, the events of September 11th were analogous to an earthquake. Though I have experienced earthquakes in California and Japan, the Loma Prieta Earthquake of 1989 really shook me. What surprised me more than the initial shaking were the long aftershocks. The lesson being that aftershocks can be more devastating than the initial quake. On this fateful day, not only were American civilians hijacked and killed in planes and in buildings, but people of many nationalities and religions lost their lives. Our sense of security, trust, and openness, all part of the American way, were hijacked. Not only that, the religion of Islam with its billion plus adherents was also hijacked.

The tragedy of September 11 has afforded both Muslims and those of other faiths a platform to discuss the usually avoided subject of religion. Personally, it has allowed me to do something I have long procrastinated in doing. To invite my neighbors to my home, my co-workers to lunch, and the community to the mosque. In doing so, I have received invaluable feedback and found many voids which have led to this book.

In order to pave the way to a better understanding of Islam and Muslims, I am leveraging the work that people have already done, where possible using positive and inspirational essays and poems.

I hope in the process that I can help demystify Islam and two of the greatest myths that exist: Jihad, which is usually misconstrued as Holy War, and the position of women in Islam, who are perceived as oppressed in a male dominated society.

This book cannot explain everything there is to know about Islam or address the ever-growing list of myths and stereotypes that are out there. I hope Islam 101 will be a primer, explaining basic concepts and tying them in with the realities of Jihad and status of women. If you want to learn more about Islam, I recommend that you get in touch with a local Islamic Center, Mosque, or a practicing Muslim who can address your questions and concerns. May God allow this little effort to benefit those who read it, to open hearts and minds, and to help build bridges of understanding, love and compassion not only here in America but throughout the world.

Javed Mohammed
Milpitas, CA

I am a Muslim

Anonymous

I am a Muslim
And God I praise
For all his blessings
My voice I raise

In one God I believe
No equal has He
of the Universe
Compassionate to me

Muhammad the Prophet
Taught me the way
To be honest and truthful
Throughout every day

The Holy Quran
To life is my guide
Its teachings I follow
By it I abide

Islam is my religion
Preaches good deeds
Mercy and Kindness
To the right path it leads

Upon all humanity
God showers his grace
Regardless of color
Nationality or race

Through working together
Our hopes increase
To live in a world
Full of love and peace

I am a Muslim
And God I praise
For all His blessings
My voice I raise

INTRODUCTION

A time to reflect a time to heal

Did you know that there are more than a billion Muslims in the world? That one of every five people on the planet is a Muslim? That Islam is the fastest growing religion on both sides of the Atlantic, in North America and Western Europe? Muslims have a history of being a part of the American and European landscape, and today they are your neighbors and co-workers, teachers and students. For the vast majority of people Islam is a stranger, perceived as a threat, envisioned as violent, and enshrouded in myths. Yet there are those who see what Islam has to offer. Islam 101 is an objective introduction to Islam, the goal being to let you judge, by reading, meeting, and understanding the faith and it's people. You don't have to agree with everything that is written. All that's asked is, as the Quran says, to come to a common ground:

"Say: O People of the Book! Come to common terms as between us and you; that we worship none but Allah (God); that we associate no partners with Him; that we erect not from ourselves lords and patrons other than Allah." (3:64)

Today there is a need for us to find this common ground, as times of crisis can bring out the best in humanity as well as the worst. After one of the worst attacks on the United States in our history, it is time for us to reflect and time for us to heal. It's a time to reaffirm our strengths and to think about our weaknesses. It's a time to understand the real threats and to identify the boundless opportunities that lie ahead of us. Those who committed and were behind the terrorist acts of September 11 were not only enemies of America, but also of Islam.

I say as both an American and as a Muslim we must have reason for hope. All the major beliefs teach that the heavens and earth all belong to God, and God is Just. Hope, trust, peace, justice, and tolerance, these are all themes that can only be achieved by going back to what we as humans have in common. In the Abrahamic traditions of Judaism, Christianity, and Islam, and also in the traditions of Hinduism and Buddhism, we find common ground and it is these themes that this book explores.

What are the commonalities that we have as human beings? We all have similar needs and wants: the needs of food, shelter, a spiritual anchor in belief, and the right of self-determination.

Hopefully you will discover that Islam is a religion through which people achieve tranquility by submitting to the one God, whose Arabic name is Allah. It is the same God as that of the prophets Abraham, Moses, and Jesus. Islam is a multi-dimensional religion which encompasses all aspects of life. It is not one entity that can be described with an adjective here and there. That Muslims believe that Islam is a peaceful religion, that Muhammad is the last prophet for humanity, and that its message is inclusive for all. Just as America is not only Hollywood, its foreign policy, or just the President, Islam is more than a religion; it is a complete way of life.

You will also discover, as in any religion, Muslims adhere to their faith at different levels. From the practicing to the non-practicing, they do not fit neatly into one box. One who declares and is witnessed as saying "There is no God but Allah and Prophet Muhammad is His Messenger," becomes a Muslim. Within the fold of Islam there are core beliefs and practices that all adherents must subscribe to, but beyond that the people and the lands that it traverses come in every color and from every culture reflecting the diversity of mankind.

There are between five and eight million Muslims in the Unites States and 12-15 million Muslims in Western Europe. The vast majority of Muslims are not anti-American or anti-democracy or anti-freedom. Many of those who show anger or protest do so as a result of their circumstances. In some cases these are common symbols of any people who fight for the right of self-determination. Hopefully this book and your interaction with Muslims will illustrate that there is a clear distinction that needs to be made between terrorists (of any faith) and those who truly practice that faith. Muslims are positive assets, law-abiding citizens, and productive members of the communities within which they live and work.

Did you know that Muslims have made some major contributions to science and civilization over the centuries? Did you know that Muslims introduced Europe to the concept of "zero" and that our numbering system is Arabic (see the resemblance below).

Did you know the origins of the science and the actual words algebra to alchemy, astronomy to the algorithm are from the Muslim world? That Muslims developed the first check? That Averroes (Ibn Rusd) transmitted and expanded on the Philosophy of Aristotle and that Avicenna (Ibn Sina) wrote the Canon of Medicine. It's not only in the sciences and mathematics, but also in art and architecture that Muslims have made profound contributions.

As issues that concern Muslims come to the world stage, we must develop a culture of dialog where we begin to understand each other. The media taints our world-views of each other and the images in our minds. It will require a conscious effort to fight the negative stereotypes that equate Islam with fundamentalism, terrorism, subjugation of women and the other misperceptions.

There is too much at stake and we have too much in common

to allow a culture of hate and misunderstanding to become embedded in our psyches. A climate of understanding and dialog needs to be fostered and the underlying issues need to be addressed in just ways. Muslims for their part need to look and reflect on the events of the past century and understand how we got into this state and how to get out, without playing the blame game. Not only does it take two to tango, but also it takes two to be tolerant, two to converse, and two to understand. September 11th has taught us many lessons and of the most important, is that we all live in a interconnected political, economical and social village.

This book will address the basics of Islam, including its beliefs and practices. It addresses some of the major myths that exist regarding the status of women and Jihad, and hopefully dispels them. You will find that most Muslims are not Arabs and that not all Arabs are Muslim. Islamic schools (Madrasahs) teach the Quran and traditions of the Prophet Muhammad, not warfare or hijacking planes. It is the exception and not the norm for Muslim men to have more than one wife. Islam came to liberate women and give them rights which most women in the West only received in the last century.

The section on September 11th, Peace and Justice is a collection of quotes, essays, and speeches which describe how both Muslims and those of other faiths view the events, and some of the outreach that has come from this tragic event.

The section on Bridge Building looks upon commonalties between the different faiths and Islam. Narratives and stories includes stories with humor and morals as well as inspirational quotes. This is followed by the personal stories of how Americans from different backgrounds became Muslim demonstrating that there are many good things about Islam which most people are not aware of. The appendices contain useful references.

Let the journey begin...

There was once a civilization...says HP CEO Carly Fiorina

There was once a civilization that was the greatest in the world. It was able to create a continental super-state that stretched from ocean to ocean, and from northern climes to tropics and deserts. Within its dominion lived hundreds of millions of people, of different creeds and ethnic origins.

One of its languages became the universal language of much of the world, the bridge between the peoples of a hundred lands. Its armies were made up of people of many nationalities, and its military protection allowed a degree of peace and prosperity that had never been known. The reach of this civilization's commerce extended from Latin America to China, and everywhere in between.

And this civilization was driven more than anything, by invention. Its architects designed buildings that defied gravity. Its mathematicians created the algebra and algorithms that would enable the building of computers, and the creation of encryption. Its doctors examined the human body, and found new cures for disease. Its astronomers looked into the heavens, named the stars, and paved the way for space travel and exploration.

Its writers created thousands of stories. Stories of courage, romance and magic. Its poets wrote of love, when others before

Dark Ages or Golden Age?

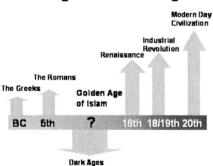

them were too steeped in fear to think of such things. When other nations were afraid of ideas, this civilization thrived on them, and kept them alive. When censors threatened to wipe out knowledge from past civilizations, this civilization kept the knowledge alive, and passed it on to others. While modern Western civilization shares many of these traits, the civilization I'm talking about was the Islamic world from the year 800 to 1600 C.E., which included the Ottoman Empire and the courts of Baghdad, Damascus and Cairo, and enlightened rulers like Suleiman the Magnificent.

Although we are often unaware of our indebtedness to this other civilization, its gifts are very much a part of our heritage. The technology industry would not exist without the contributions of Arab mathematicians. Sufi poet-philosophers like Rumi challenged our notions of self and truth. Leaders like Suleiman contributed to our notions of tolerance and civic leadership.

And perhaps we can learn a lesson from his example: It was leadership based on meritocracy, not inheritance. It was leadership that harnessed the full capabilities of a very diverse population--that included Christianity, Islamic, and Jewish traditions.

This kind of enlightened leadership --leadership that nurtured culture, sustainability, diversity and courage -- led to 800 years of invention and prosperity. In dark and serious times like this, we must affirm our commitment to building societies and institutions that aspire to this kind of greatness. More than ever, we must focus on the importance of leadership-- bold acts of leadership and decidedly personal acts of leadership.

Historical Perspective by Syed Abul Ala Maududi

Islam began when man's career on earth began—more precisely at the time of man's creation and his descent. Allah created Adam and Eve and enjoined them to worship Him and live a life of obedience to the Divine Will.

Allah is the Creator and Sustainer of the Universe and of human beings. Man must turn to Him for sustenance and guidance. The very word Islam means obedience to God. In this respect, Islam is man's natural religion—the only natural course is for man to look towards Him for guidance.

The day Adam and Eve were sent down to live on earth,

Allah told them that they were His servants and He was their Master and Creator. He told them and mankind that the best course was for them to follow His guidance, to obey His orders, and to refrain from what He had forbidden. God said to them that He would be pleased if they obeyed Him and in turn He would reward them. If, however, they did not heed His commands, He would be displeased and would punish them. This was the simple beginning of Islam.

Adam and Eve invited their children to follow the Islamic way of life. They and their children and their later generations followed the teachings of Islam as propounded by Prophet Adam for quite a long period of time. It was only later that certain people began disobeying Allah. Some of them began worshipping other gods of their own making, some of them regarded themselves as gods, while a few others even declared their freedom to do as they pleased—defying God's orders. This is how disbelief came into being. Its essence lies in refusal to worship God—pursuing the path of defiance to the Creator.

When disbelief began to increase and multiply it affected the life of society in a number of ways. Exploitation, oppression, viciousness and immorality emerged in different forms. Life became intolerable. Allah then appointed some righteous people to preach the Message of Truth among the wrongdoers, invite them to the Right Path and convert them to God-fearing people— worshipping and obeying God Alone.

In short, they were asked to perform a mission—to make people righteous and true Muslims. These noble people entrusted with this great mission were called Prophets or Messengers of Allah. Allah sent these prophets to different nations and countries. All of them were honest, truthful, and people of noble character. All of them preached the same religion: Islam. To mention a few names: Noah, Abraham, Moses and Jesus. All of them were the prophets of God and thousands of them were, over the centuries, sent into the world to guide mankind.

In the history of the last few thousand years, one can see the recurrent arrival of prophets. whenever disbelief increased and assumed menacing proportions. The prophets tried to stop the tide of disbelief and invited people towards Islam. Some people adopted the Islamic way of life, but others rejected it. The people who followed the prophets became Muslims and, after learning higher ethical and moral disciplines from them, began to preach and spread nobility and goodness. Having forgotten the teachings of Islam, later generations of Muslims themselves gradually sank into disbelief. Whenever such a situation arose, God sent a prophet or messenger to revive Islam. This continual arrival of messengers of God continued for thousands of years. In the course of those long years, Islam was revived by those prophets, who restated the Message forgotten by their people. At long last God sent the prophet Muhammad who revived Islam in such an outstanding fashion that it still exists today and will continue to exist (God willing), till eternity.

Basics of Islam

What is Islam and who are Muslims?

The word "Islam" is an Arabic word which means "submission to the will of God." This word comes from the same root as the Arabic word "salama," which means "peace."

The religion of Islam teaches that in order to achieve true peace of mind and surety of heart, one must submit to God and live according to His Divinely Revealed Law. The most important truth that God revealed to mankind is that there is nothing divine or worthy of being worshiped except for Almighty God, thus all human beings should submit to Him. The word Islam differs when compared to other faiths, in that it is not named after its founder (e.g. Christianity after Christ or Buddhism after Buddha), nor tribe or race (e.g. Judaism after Judah) or with the land and soil (e.g. the word Hindu is derived from the Sanskrit word sindhu ("river").

The word "Muslim" means one who submits to the will of God, regardless of their race, nationality, or ethnic background. Being a Muslim entails willful submission and active obedience to God and living in accordance with His message. Some people mistakenly believe that Islam is just a religion for Arabs, but nothing could be further from the truth. Not only are there converts to Islam in every corner of the world, especially in the United States and England, but by taking a look at the Muslim world from Chechnya to Chad, from Malaysia to Morocco, one can see clearly that Muslims come from many different races, ethnic groups and nationalities. It is also interesting to note that more than 80% of all Muslims are non Arabs. There are more Muslims in the Indian sub-continent than in the whole Arab world! So even though it is true that most Arabs are Muslims, the large majority of Muslims are not Arabs.

Every phenomenon in the world is administered by laws made by God; and everything that is obedient to God and submissive to His laws is considered to be in the state of Islam. Humans possess the qualities of intelligence and choice, thus they are invited to submit to the guidance of God and obey His law, and therefore become a Muslim. Submission to the will of God, together with obedience to His beneficial law, is the best safeguard for peace and harmony.

Islam dates back to the age of Adam and its message has been conveyed to human kind by God's prophets and messengers including Abraham, Moses, Jesus and Muhammad. Islam's message has been restored and enforced in the final stage of the religious evolution by God's last prophet and messenger Muhammad.

Who is Allah and what do Muslims believe about Allah?

The Oneness of God

The word Allah in the Arabic language means "The God," the One and Only Eternal God, Creator of the Universe. The Most Compassionate, and the Most Merciful are two of the 99 most beautiful attributes of God.

The foundation of the Islamic faith is belief in the Oneness of the Almighty God, the God of Abraham, Noah, Moses and Jesus. Islam teaches that a pure belief in One God is intuitive in human beings and thus fulfills the natural inclination of the soul. According to the teachings of Islam, Almighty God is absolutely

One and His Oneness should never be compromised by associating partners with Him, neither in worship nor in belief. Due to this, Muslims are required to maintain a direct relationship with God; therefore, all intermediaries are absolutely forbidden; all prayer and worship are exclusively for God.

It is interesting to note that the word Allah for God is also used by Arabic speaking Jews and Christians. This is because "Allah" is the only word in the Arabic language equivalent to the English word "God." Additionally, the Arabic word "Allah" cannot be made plural or given gender (i.e. masculine or feminine), which goes hand-in-hand with the Islamic concept of God. When God is referred to as He or Him, this is a nuance of the language.

So what do Muslims believe about Allah? The following often recited chapter summarizes who God is?

"Say: He Allah, is One. Allah is He on Whom all depend. He begets not, nor is he begotten. And none is like Him (112:1-4)

The following are some further details:

1. Allah is the one God, Who has no partner.

2. Nothing is like Him. He is the Creator, not created, nor a part of His creation.

3. He is All-Powerful, absolutely Just.

4. Allah knows what is in our hearts.

5. There is no other entity in the entire universe worthy of worship besides Him.

6. He is First, Last, and Everlasting; He existed when there was nothing and will exist when nothing else remains.

7. He is the All-Knowing and All Merciful, the Supreme, the Sovereign.

8. It is only He who is capable of granting life to anything.

9. He sent His messengers to guide all of mankind, including Muhammad as the last prophet and messenger

10. His final revelation is the Holy Quran, the only revealed book in the world in its authentic form.

Why Islam?

What are some of these basic characteristics which have given Islam such a large following? Muslims believe the message of

Islam is for all human beings and relevant for all time. Its teachings and authenticity have been preserved. The message of Islam is a return to pure monotheism, the belief in One God who alone is worthy of worship. It is simple and free from superstitions. This message is for the entire human race and reminds humanity that Allah is the God of all the worlds. It reaffirms the previous prophets and completes the faith in the prophethood of Muhammad. Islam awakens in the human the faculty of reason and impresses upon humans the need to use our intellect and observation to know the Creator and Creation.

Faith also is not a mere profession of beliefs, but righteous conduct has to follow, and accountability is made clear with the belief in life after death. Islam establishes a balance between individualism and collectivism; believing in the individual and holding everyone personally accountable to God.

Islam breaks down barriers such as nationality, race, class, and color and unites humanity under one banner. It addresses the elements of permanence and change, giving any society in any time and space the demands of stability and growth.

Islam spread far and wide due to its tolerance of other beliefs. Islamic law protects the privileged status of minorities, and this is one reason why churches, synagogues, temples and other places of worship have flourished all over the Islamic world. It also awakens a sense of social responsibility to benefit society.

Ultimately the question is not "Why Islam?" Those that see the benefits that Islam can bring to humanity ask "Why not Islam?"

What is the Quran?

The Arabic world "Al-Quran" (sometimes spelled Koran) literally means "the recitation." When used in regards to Islam, the word refers to God's final message to mankind that was revealed to the Prophet Muhammad. According to Muslim belief, the Quran has been preserved in its words, pronunciation, and meaning and is believed to be the literal word of God. The Quran is a living miracle in the Arabic language and is known to be inimitable in its style, form, and spiritual impact. It is "a guidance to the people and clear signs of guidance and the criterion between

right and wrong." (2:185)

The Quran was revealed to the Prophet Muhammad over a period of 23 years and is believed by Muslims to be the Word of God. The Quran was recited publicly during the life of the Prophet Muhammad. Numerous companions of the Prophet memorized the entire Quran word-for-word as it was revealed. The Quran has been memorized generation after generation, preserved for anyone who wants access to it.

Regarding the teachings of the Quran, its message is addressed to all humanity. The fundamental message that it brings is the same message of all of the prophets, "submit to Almighty God and worship Him alone." As such, God's revelation in the Quran focuses on teaching human beings the importance of believing in the Unity of God and framing their lives around the guidance which He has sent. The Quran contains stories of the previous prophets, such as Abraham, Noah, Moses and Jesus; as well as many commands and prohibitions from God. In modern times, in which so many people are caught up in doubt, spiritual despair, and "political correctness," the Quranic teachings offer solutions to the emptiness of our lives and the turmoil that is gripping the world. The impact of this book is such that Allah says:

"Had We revealed this Quran upon a mountain, surely you would have seen it humble itself and crumble out of the fear of Allah. Such are the parables We put forward to mankind so that they may reflect." (59:21)

Other Scriptures

Besides the Quran the other books that were revealed are:

1) The Torah, which was revealed to Moses, peace be upon him. It is the greatest among the Israelites' books: "Surely, We sent down the Torah, wherein is guidance and light; by its laws the Jews have been judged by the prophets who surrendered themselves to Allah, the rabbis and the doctors of law, because they were entrusted the protection of Allah's book and were witnesses there to." (5:44).

2) The Gospel (Bible) which was revealed to Jesus. It is a con-

firmation of the Torah and a complement to it: "And we gave him the Gospel, wherein is guidance and light and confirming the Torah before it, as a guidance and an admonition to the God-fearing." (5:46); "And to make lawful to you certain things that, before, were forbidden to you." (3:50).

3) The Psalms, which Allah gave to David, peace be upon him.

4) The Tablets of Abraham and Moses, peace be upon them.

Sample Verses from the Holy Quran

(Please note the Quran is a book whose true form is in Arabic. The following are at best translation and interpretation of the verses.)

Oneness of God

"Allah! There is no god but He, the Ever-living, the Self-subsisting, Eternal. No slumber can seize Him nor sleep. His are all things in the heavens and on earth. Who is there that can intercede in His presence except by His permission? He knows what is before them and what is behind them, and they cannot comprehend anything out of His knowledge except what He pleases. His knowledge extends over the heavens and the earth, and the preservation of them both tires Him not, and He is the most High, the Great." (2:255)

Belief and Righteousness

"It is not righteousness that ye turn your faces towards the East or West; but it is righteousness to believe in Allah and the Last Day, and the Angels, and the Book, and the Messengers; to spend of your substance, out of love for Him, for your kin, for orphans, for the needy, for the wayfarer, for those who ask, and for the ransom of slaves; to be steadfast in prayer, and practice regular charity; to fulfill the contracts which ye have made; and to be firm and patient, in pain (or suffering) and adversity, and throughout all periods of panic. Such are the people of truth, the God-fearing." (2:177)

God-Consciousness (Taqwa)

"It is He Who has created for you (the faculties of) hearing, sight, feeling, and understanding: little thanks is it you give! And He has multiplied you through the earth, and to Him shall ye be gathered back. It is He Who gives life and death, and to Him (is due) the alteration of Night and Day: will ye not then understand?

On the contrary they say things similar to what the ancients said. They say: "What! when we die and become dust and bones, could we really be raised up again? Such things have been promised to us and to our fathers before! they are nothing but tales of the ancients!

Say: Whose is the earth, and whoever is therein, if you know? They will say: Allah's. Say: Will you not then mind? Say Who is the Lord of the seven heavens and the Lord of the mighty dominion? They will say: (This is) Allah's. Say: Will you not then guard (against evil)? Say: Who is it in Whose hand is the kingdom of all things and Who gives help, but against Whom help is not given, if you but do know?"(23:78-88)

Among His Signs

"Among His Signs is this, that He created you from dust; and then,-- behold, ye are men scattered (far and wide)!

And among His Signs is this, that He created for you mates from among yourselves, that ye may dwell in tranquility with them, and He has put love and mercy between your (hearts): verily in that are Signs for those who reflect.

And among His Signs is the creation of the heavens and the earth, and the variations in your languages and your colors. Verily in that are Signs for those who know.

And among His Signs is the sleep that ye take by night and by day, and the quest that ye (make for livelihood) out of His Bounty: verily in that are signs for those who hearken.

And among His Signs, He shows you the lightning, by way both of fear and of hope, and He sends down rain from the sky and with it gives life to the earth after it is dead: verily in that are Signs for those who are wise.

And among His Signs is this, that heaven and earth stand by His

19

Command: then when He calls you, by a single call, from the earth, behold, ye (straightway) come forth. To Him belongs every being that is in the heavens and on earth: all are devoutly obedient to Him. It is He Who begins (the process of) creation; then repeats it; and for Him it is most easy. To Him belongs the loftiest similitude (we can think of) in the heavens and the earth: for He is Exalted in Might, full of wisdom." (30:20-27)

Resurrection

"O people! if ye have a doubt about the Resurrection, (consider) that We created you out of dust, then out of sperm, then out of a leech-like clot, then out of a morsel of flesh, partly formed and partly unformed, in order that We may manifest (our power) to you; and We cause whom We will to rest in the wombs for an appointed term, then do We bring you out as babies, then (foster you) that ye may reach your age of full strength; and some of you are called to die, and some are sent back to the feeblest old age, so that they know nothing after having known (much).

And (further), thou see the earth barren and lifeless, but when We pour down rain on it, it is stirred (to life), it swells, and it puts forth every kind of beautiful growth (in pairs). This is so, because Allah is the Reality: it is He Who gives life to the dead, and it is He Who has power over all things. And verily the Hour will come: there can be no doubt about it, or about (the fact) that Allah will raise up all who are in the graves." (22:5-7)

Success and Qualities of a Believer

"Successful indeed are the believers. Those who humble themselves in their prayers. Who avoid vain talk. Who are active in deeds of charity. And who guard their modesty. Except before their mates or those whom their right hands possess, for they surely are not blameworthy. But whoever seeks to go beyond that, these are they that exceed the limits. Those who faithfully observe their trusts and their covenants; And who pay heed to their prayers. These will be the heirs, who will inherit paradise. There they will abide." (23:1-11)

Wisdom and Advice of Loqman to his Son

"O my son! keep up prayer and enjoin the good and forbid the evil and bear patiently that which befalls you; surely these acts require courage. And do not turn your face away from people in contempt, nor go about in the land exulting overmuch; surely Allah does not love any self-conceited boaster; And pursue the right course in your going about and lower your voice; surely the most hateful of voices is the braying of the asses." (31:17-19)

Parents, Neighbors and Rights of Others

"Treat with kindness your parents and kindred and orphans and those in need; speak fair to the people; be steadfast in prayer; and practice regular charity. (2:83)

Thy Lord hath decreed that ye worship none but Him, and that ye be kind to your parents. Whether one or both of them attain old age in thy life, say not to them a word of contempt, nor repel them, but address them in terms of honor. And, out of kindness, lower to them the wing of humility, and say: "My Lord! Bestow on them Thy Mercy even as they cherished me in childhood." (17:23-24)

"Serve Allah and join not any partners with Him; and do good to parents, kinsfolk, orphans, those in need, neighbors who are near, neighbors who are strangers, the companion by your side, the wayfarer (ye meet), and what your right hands possess: for Allah loves not the arrogant, the vainglorious." (4:36)

Greetings

"And when those who believe in Our communications come to you, say: Peace be on you, your Lord has ordained mercy on Himself, (so) that if any one of you does evil in ignorance, then turns after that and acts aright, then He is Forgiving, Merciful." (6:54)

Co-operation

"O you who believe! Do not violate the signs appointed by Allah nor the sacred month, nor (interfere with) the offerings, nor the sacrificial animals with garlands, nor those going to the sacred house seeking the grace and pleasure of their Lord; and when you are free from the obligations of the pilgrimage, then hunt, and let not hatred of a people— because they hindered you from the Sacred Masjid— incite you to exceed the limits, and help one another in goodness and piety, and do not help one another in sin and aggression; and be careful of (your duty to) Allah; surely Allah is severe in requiting (evil)." (5:2)

Promises

"Fulfill the promise; surely (every) promise shall be questioned about." (17:34)

Truthfulness

"Surely the men who submit and the women who submit, and the believing men and the believing women, and the obeying men and the obeying women, and the truthful men and the truthful women, and the patient men and the patient women and the humble men and the humble women, and the almsgiving men and the almsgiving women, and the fasting men and the fasting women, and the men who guard their private parts and the women who guard, and the men who remember Allah much and the women who remember— Allah has prepared for them forgiveness and a mighty reward." (33:35)

Patience

"O you who believe! Seek assistance through patience and prayer; surely Allah is with the patient. And do not speak of those who are slain in Allah's way as dead; nay, (they are) alive, but you do not perceive. And We will most certainly try you with somewhat of fear and hunger and loss of property and lives and fruits; and give good news to the patient, who, when a misfortune befalls them, say: Surely we are Allah's and to Him we shall surely return. Those are they on whom are blessings and mercy from their Lord, and those are the followers of the right course."
(2:153-157)

Justice

"O you who believe! Stand out firmly for Allah, as witnesses to fair dealing, and let not the hatred of others to you make you swerve to wrong and depart from justice. Be just: that is next to piety: and fear Allah. For Allah is well acquainted with all that ye do." (5:8)

Chastity and Covering for Women

"And say to the believing women that they should lower their gaze and guard their modesty; that they should not display their beauty and ornaments except what (must ordinarily) appear thereof; that they should draw their veils over their bosoms and not display their beauty except to their husbands, their fathers, their husband's fathers, their sons, their husbands' sons, their brothers or their brothers' sons, or their sisters' sons, or their women, or the slaves whom their right hands possess, or male servants free of physical needs, or small children who have no sense of the shame of sex; and that they should not strike their feet in order to draw attention to their hidden ornaments. And O you Believers! Turn ye all together towards Allah, that ye may attain Bliss." (24:31)

Message to People of the Book (Jews, Christians and Sabeans)

"Do no dispute with the people of the Book, unless it be in a way that is better, save with such of them as do wrong; and say: We believe in that which has been revealed unto us, and revealed unto you; our God and your God is One, and unto Him we surrender." (29:46)

"Among the people of the Book there are some who believe in God and that which is revealed unto you and that which was revealed unto them, humbling themselves before God. They do not sell the revelations of God for a trifling gain. Their reward is with their Lord, and God is swift to take account." (3:199)

Mary and Jesus

"O Mary! Allah gives thee glad tidings of a Word from Him: his name will be Christ Jesus, the son of Mary, held in honor in this world and the Hereafter and of (the company of) those nearest to Allah." (3:45)

Who is Prophet Muhammad?

The Prophet Muhammad was born an orphan in Mecca in the year 570 CE.   Since his father died before his birth and his mother when he was six, he was raised first by his grandfather and then by his uncle from the respected tribe of Quraysh. As he grew, he became known for his truthfulness, generosity and sincerity, so that he was sought after for his ability to arbitrate in disputes. The historians describe him as calm and meditative. Muhammad was of a deeply religious nature and had long detested the decadence of his society.

It became his habit to meditate from time to time in the Cave of Hira near Mecca. At the age of 40, in the year 610 CE, while engaged in a meditative retreat, prophet Muhammad was chosen by God to deliver His message of peace, namely Islam. It was in this cave that the prophet Muhammad received the first revelation, the first words of the Quran brought by the Angel Gabriel (Gibreel) to mankind:

"Read in the name of your Lord, Who Created. Created humans out of a clot of blood. Read and your Lord is the Most Bountiful. The One who taught by the pen. Taught the human that which he did not know." (Surah Al-Alaq 96:1-5)

This revelation, which continued for 23 years is known as the Quran. As soon as he began to recite the words he heard from Gabriel and to preach the truth which God had revealed to him, he and his small group of followers suffered bitter persecution which grew so fierce that in the year 622, God gave them the command to emigrate.

This event, the Hijra ('migration'), in which they left Mecca for the city of Medina, marks the beginning of the Muslim calendar. After several years, the Prophet and his followers were able to return to Mecca, where they forgave their enemies and established Islam definitively. Before the Prophet died at the age of 63, the greater part of the Arabian peninsula was Muslim and within a century of his death Islam had spread to Spain in the West and as far East as China. He died with less than 5 possessions to his name.

While Muhammad was chosen to deliver the message, he is

not considered the founder of Islam. Muslims consider Islam to be the same divine guidance sent to all peoples before. Muslims believe that the Prophet Muhammad was only a man chosen by God, and that he is not divine in any way. In order to avoid the misguided wish to deify him, the Prophet Muhammad taught Muslims to refer to him as "God's Messenger and His Servant".

Prophet Muhammad is considered to be the summation and the culmination of all the prophets and messengers that came before him. He confirmed the previous messages and completed the Message of God for all humanity. He was entrusted with the power of explaining, interpreting, and living the teachings of the Quran.

Muslims believe all the prophets from Adam, Noah, Moses, Jesus etc. were all sent with divine guidance for their peoples. Every prophet was sent to his own people, but Muhammad was sent to all of mankind. Muhammad is the last and final messenger sent to deliver the message of Islam. Muslims revere and honor him for all he went through and his dedication, but they do not worship him.

"O Prophet, verily We have sent you as a witness and a bearer of glad tidings and a warner and as one who invites unto God by His leave and as an illuminating lamp."(33:45-6)

The Prophet says of his role with respect to the previous prophets, "To compare me with the other prophets, suppose a man built a house, completing and perfecting it but for the space of one brick. People would go around it, admiring its beauty and saying," But for the space of one brick…Well I am that brick!" So Islam confirms all the traditions that went before it.

The final prophet of Islam lived in the full light of history and the minutest details of his life are known. Not only do Muslims have the complete text of God's words that were revealed to Prophet Muhammad, but they have also preserved his saying and teachings in what are called "hadith" literature. Whereas, the Quran is the word of Allah, the Traditions of Prophet Muhammad are the practical interpretations of the Quran.

The mission of the last and final prophet of God was to teach that "there is nothing divine or worthy of being worshiped except for Almighty God," as well as being a living example of God's revelation. In simple terms, God sent the revelation to Prophet

Muhammad, who in turn taught it, preached it, lived it, and put it into practice. In this way, Prophet Muhammad was more than just a "prophet" in the sense of many of the Biblical prophets, since he was also a statesman and ruler. He was a man who lived a humble life in the service of God and established an all-encompassing religion and way of life by showing what it means to be an ideal friend, husband, teacher, ruler, warrior, and judge. For this reason, Muslims follow him not for his own sake, but in obedience to God, because Prophet Muhammad not only showed people how to deal with our fellow human beings, but more importantly, he showed them how to relate to God. The Prophet Muhammad practiced and taught universal equality and this is demonstrated in how far and wide Islam has spread.

Like other prophets, Prophet Muhammad faced a great deal of opposition and persecution during his mission. However, he was always patient and just, even to his enemies. His mission started in one of the most backward places on earth, but within a hundred years of his death, Islam had spread from Spain to China. The Prophet Muhammad is considered the greatest of all of God's prophets, not because he had new doctrines or greater miracles, but because the results of his mission have brought more human beings into the pure and proper belief in the One True God than any other prophet.

The Prophet Muhammad was a mercy to mankind and the ideal role model. The Quran verifies this:

"And We have not sent you except as a mercy to mankind" (21:107)

"Indeed in the messenger of Allah you have the most beautiful pattern of conduct for him who hopes in Allah and the Last Day, and remembers Allah much." (33:21)

Selections from the Sayings of the Prophet Muhammed

Mercy, Compassion, and Rights of Human Beings

"God has no mercy for him who has no mercy for his fellow human beings".

"Visit the sick, feed the hungry, and help to relieve people's misery".

"He who eases the hardship of another, will have ease bestowed upon him by God in this world and the next... God goes on helping a servant so long as he goes on helping his fellow-man."

Faith, Fanaticism, and Jihad

"God is Gentle and loves gentleness in all things."

"There is a polish for everything and the polish for the heart is the remembrance of God."

"Faith is to restrain oneself against all violence, let no believer commit any violence."

Someone asked the Prophet what fanaticism was and he replied: "That you help your people in wrongdoing."

Someone said: "O Prophet of God, teach me something." "Abuse no one," replied the Prophet, and despise not anything good and speak to your fellow men with open countenance."

Family

"Honor your children (especially daughters) and make provisions for their proper up-bringing."

"One who brings up three daughters, teaches them good manners and morals, helps them get married, and treats them with fairness will earn Paradise."

"The most perfect of believers in the matter of faith is he whose behavior is best; and the best of you are those who behave best towards their wives."

"A man came seeking permission to participate in battle. The Prophet asked him: "Are your parents alive?" The man said: "Yes." He sent him away saying: "Then go back and find your jihad in serving them."

"Paradise lies at the feet of your mother."

"You will not enter Paradise until you have faith, and you will not complete you faith until you love one another."

Neighbors

1. "He is not a believer who eats his fill while his neighbor goes without food."

2. Rights of a neighbor: a list of rights from the Prophet Muhammad:

"Help them when they need help, give them support if they ask for it, lend them things that they need, visit them from time to time, don't hurt them, even if they hurt you, visit them when they are ill, be happy for their good luck, be kind to them when they have bad luck, attend their funeral if they die, share your food with them, and do not bother them."

Animal Rights

"You will be rewarded by God for your acts of kindness towards all living creatures."

Manners and Conduct

Truthfulness, Tolerance and Thankfulness

"Guarantee me six things and I shall assure you of Paradise: when you speak, speak the truth, keep your promise, discharge your trust, guard your chastity, lower your gaze, and withhold your hands from highhandedness."

"He who does not thank people does not thank Allah."

"There are two rails in me which Allah likes, toleration and deliberation in undertakings."

Intention and Action

"Actions shall be judged only by intention, a person will get what they intend."

"Every good action is a charity and it is a good action to meet a friend with a smiling face."

Knowledge, Wealth and the Good Life

" The seeking of knowledge is a must for every Muslim man and woman."

"Wealth does not come from abundance of goods but from a contended heart."

" Eat and drink, give charity and wear good clothes as long as these do not involve excess or arrogance."

Suspicion, Jealousy, Anger, and Pride

"Beware of suspicion, for suspicion may be based on false information, do not spy on another, do not disclose others hidden defects."

" Keep away from jealousy for as fire burns wood, so jealousy consumes good actions."

" He is not strong who throws down another, but he is who controls his anger."

"If anyone has got an atom of pride in his heart, he will not enter Paradise."

Forgiveness

"God Most High said, 'O Son of Adam, as long as you call on Me and place your hope in Me, I forgive you what you have done, no matter how much. Son of Adam, even if your sins pile up to the clouds in the sky, if you then call on Me for forgiveness I will forgive you. Son of Adam, if you come to me with an earth full of sins, you will meet Me without associating anything with Me, I will come to you with that much forgiveness.' "

The World

"The world is a prison for the believer, a paradise for the non-believer"

Mindfulness

" Be mindful of God, and you will find God in front of you. Acknowledge God in ease and God will acknowledge you in distress. And know that what misleads you will never enable you to do right and what enables you to do right will never mislead you. And know that help comes with patience, and relief comes with distress; and that with difficulty comes ease."

Mercy

"God rendered Mercy into a hundred parts, keeping ninety-nine parts and sending one part down to earth. By virtue of that one portion, creatures are merciful to one another, such that the mares lifts her hooves away from her foal, fearing she may step on it."

"Whoever is not merciful will not be shown mercy."

Help

"Help your brother, whether he be an oppressor or one of the oppressed."

Some said, ", O Messenger of God, we help him if he is the oppressed, but how can we help him if he is an oppressor? " The Prophet said, "By stopping him."

Jesus and Muhammad

The Prophet said," I am the closest of all people to Jesus, son of Mary, in this world and in the Hereafter; for all the prophets are brothers, with different mothers but one religion."

Hercules and what was said about Muhammad

To discover a person, it is good not only to see what they spoke as was covered in the sayings of Muhammad, but it's also good to see what those who opposed him said. Abu Sufian, the leader of the pagan Meccans and one of Islam's bitterest enemies happened to be in Jerusalem at the same time as Heraclius (Hercules), the Roman Emperor. Hercules wanted to find an Arab from Mecca who he could question about Muhammad. Abu Sufian was brought with his friends to the presence of the Emperor and the following conversation took place.

Heraclius: "Do you know this man, Muhammad, who sent me a message claiming to be a Prophet? Can you say what sort of family he comes from?"

Abu Sufian:	"He comes from a noble family."
Heraclius:	"Have any of his forefathers been a king?"
Abu Sufian:	"No"
Heraclius:	"Has there been anyone from his family who has made claims similar to this?"
Abu Sufian:	"No"
Heraclius:	"Are the people who have accepted his religion poor or rich?"
Abu Sufian:	"They are poor."
Heraclius:	"Do his followers increase or decrease?"
Abu Sufian:	"They increase."
Heraclius:	"Did you accuse him of falsehood before he made that claim?"
Abu Sufian:	"No. We have never known him to tell a lie."

31

Heraclius:	"Does he ever go against his covenants?"
Abu Sufian:	"Not so far, but we have to see whether he will carry out the new agreement between ourselves and him."
Heraclius:	"Have you ever fought him in war?"
Abu Sufian:	"Yes"
Heraclius:	"What was the outcome?"
Abu Sufian:	"Sometimes we won, and sometimes he won."
Heraclius:	"What does he teach?"
Abu Sufian:	"He teaches the people to worship one God, and not set up equals to Him, to be chaste, to speak only the truth, and always to adjure all vicious and corrupt practices. He exhorts the people to be good to one another and to keep their covenants and discharge their trusts."

Heraclius then commented on his questions and explained to Abu Sufian why he had asked them.

"You say he is of noble birth; prophets are always of noble birth. You say his family has never claimed prophet-hood before. If it had been so, I would have thought that he was doing so now under the influence of heredity. You admit that there has been no king in his family, if it had been so, I would have thought he was after a crown. You acknowledge that he does not lie. He who does not lie to men, how can he lie to God? You witness that poor people follow him. It is always the poor who follow prophets, before others. You say he does not break his promises. Prophets never deceive. You say he teaches: prayers, piety and chastity. If all this were true, I am sure his kingdom will reach the place where I stand. I was sure that a Prophet was coming, but I did not think he would be born in Arabia. I wish I were with Muhammad to wash his feet.

Abu Sufian then left telling his people that Muhammad's position had risen high. Heraclius is known to have gathered his people and recognized that Muhammad was a prophet sent by God and asked his people to follow the Prophet. They declined, seeing that their kingdom and wealth was greater.

The Purpose of Life: Status and Salvation

Muslims believe that human beings enjoy an especially high ranking status in the hierarchy of all known creatures. Human beings occupy this distinguished position because they alone are gifted with rational faculties and spiritual aspirations as well as powers of action. They are the most dignified creation potentially capable of good and noble achievements.

Islam teaches that every person is born in a state of purity (fitrah). God endows every person with the spiritual potential and intellectual inclination that can make him or her a good Muslim. Every person's birth takes place according to the will of God in realization of His plans and in submission to His commands. Every person is born free from sin. When the person reaches the age of maturity and if they are sane, they become accountable for all their deeds and intentions. Humans are free from sin until they commit a sin.

Muslims believe that the purpose of life is to worship God. This does not mean spending entire lives in constant seclusion and absolute meditation. To worship God is to know Him, to love Him, to obey His commands, and to enforce His laws in every aspect of life. Also to serve His cause by doing right and shunning evil, and to be just to ourselves and to our fellow human beings.

Faith is not complete when it is followed blindly or accepted unquestioningly. A person must build his or her faith on well-grounded convictions beyond any reasonable doubt. Islam ensures freedom to believe and forbids compulsion in religion (some of the oldest synagogues and oldest churches in the world are in Muslim countries).

Humans must work out their salvation through the guidance of God, according to the Islamic creed. No one can act on behalf of another or intercede between him or her and God. In order to obtain salvation, a person must combine faith and action, belief and practice. Allah does not hold any person responsible until he has shown him or her the right way. If people do not know and have no way of knowing about Islam, they will not be responsible for failing to be Muslim. Every Muslim must invite to Islam in words and be exemplary in actions.

How did Islam Spread and to Where?

When the prophet Muhammad emigrated from Mecca to Medina, he established the foundation for a Muslim state. From Medina, Muslim rule expanded throughout the Arab Peninsula. After the death of the prophet Muhammad in 632CE, the leadership was passed serially on to the Caliphs Abu Bakr, Omar, Usman, and Ali, who were all companions of the Prophet. As Muslims embarked on campaigns to spread the faith, delegations and armies were sent into North Africa and to the East. As there is no compulsion in faith, in accordance with a Quranic injunction, the people either had the choice of accepting Islam or paying a tax. The tax exempted them from participating in the military. Islam reached North Africa and Spain to the west, Syria, Palestine and Turkey to the north, Persia, India and as far as China and Indonesia in the east. Muslim empires had their capitals in cities like Damascus, Baghdad, Istanbul, Granada, Samarkand, and Delhi. At various points in time these empires declined due to internal weakness and strong opposition first from the Mongols, and then the European Crusades, and finally colonization. The key point to emphasize is that Islam was not and cannot be spread by the sword, which is a common myth.

What is Islamic Law?

Islamic law, Shariah, is a comprehensive legal system which covers all aspects of life from personal to civil, criminal to con-

World Muslim Population

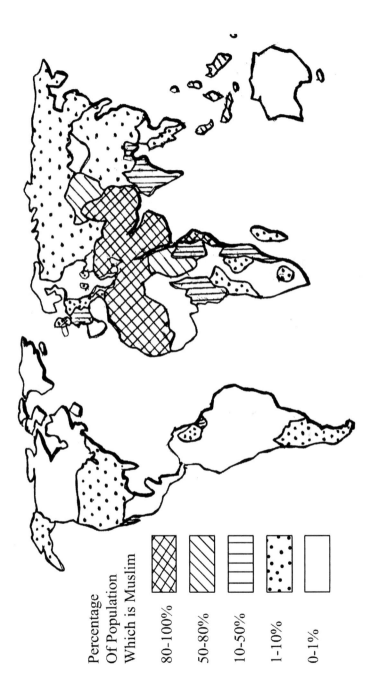

Percentage
Of Population
Which is Muslim

80-100%

50-80%

10-50%

1-10%

0-1%

stitutional, and social to cultural. The Quran and the Prophetic traditions are the primary sources of Islamic law. Whereas the Quran is a revealed text whose authenticity has been guaranteed by God according to Muslim belief, the traditions of the Prophet were compiled by his companions. The Quran in some cases is very specific and in others general in nature, so the Prophetic traditions provide the details. For example, the Quran commands the believers to pray but it is the Sunnah and Hadith that provides the details of how to pray.

The Traditions were collected and verified through a systematic process of recording the chain of narrators all the way back to the Prophet. The two most famous collections of narrations are by the scholars Imam Bukhari and Imam Muslim.

Next in degree comes the Ijma, which is the consensus of opinion of scholars, and Qiyas, which are laws, derived through analogy. These are required when the Quran and Prophetic traditions do not address specific new situations or problems. However, the general principles are still derived from the Quran and the Sunnah/Hadith.

The beliefs and practices of Islam are based on the articles of faith and the five pillars respectively. What follows is a narrated story about the Prophet Muhammad, which summarizes Islam's beliefs and practices as well as the ascending levels of faith. Following this, each article of faith and belief is further explained.

Beliefs and practices of Islam

The 3 levels of Belief
(Faith, Submission, and Goodness)

One day the Prophet was sitting with some people when the archangel Gabriel came to him and said

"What is submission?" The Prophet replied, "Submission is to testify there is no God but Allah and Muhammad is His Messenger, to pray regularly, to pay the prescribed welfare tax, to fast in the month of Ramadan and to make the Pilgrimage if one can do so." "What is faith", asked the angel?. The Prophet replied, "Faith is to believe in God, His angels, His books, His messengers, the last day and to believe in divine destiny." Gabriel asked, "What is goodness?" The Prophet replied, "To worship God as if you actually see God; for if you do not see God, God certainly sees you."

Articles of Faith

The articles of faith, to believe in Allah, His Messengers, and revelations have already been detailed in the previous section. The following are the remaining articles of faith:

The Angels

Muslims believe angels were created from light by God. They require no food, drink or sleep. They have no physical desires, free will, or material needs. Angels spend their time in the service of Allah. Each is charged with a certain duty. Angels cannot be seen by the naked eye. Belief in the angels is part of the realm known as "the unseen."

The Day of Judgment

Belief in the Day of Judgment (Akhira) is a fundamental tenant of Islam. This world as we know it will come to an end. On that day, all men and women, from Adam to the last person, will be resurrected from their graves for judgment. Everything we do, say, make, intend and think is accounted for and kept in accurate records which will be brought up on the Day of Judgment.

One who believes in life after death is not expected to behave against the Will of Allah. They will always bear in mind that Allah is watching all their actions and the angels are recording them and that Allah will judge their actions.

People with good records will be generously rewarded and warmly welcomed to Allah's Heaven. People with bad records will be fairly punished and cast into Hell. Allah knows the real nature of Heaven and Hell only, but Allah describes them in terms familiar to man in the Quran.

If some good deeds are seen not to get full appreciation and credit in this life, they will receive full compensation and be widely acknowledged on the Day of Judgment. If some people who commit sins, neglect Allah and indulge in immoral activities seem superficially successful and prosperous in this life, absolute justice will be done to them on the Day of Judgment. Allah alone knows the time of the Day of Judgment.

Pre-destination

"What God grants to men out of His mercy, no one can withhold, and what He withholds no one can grant apart from Him. And He is the Powerful, the Wise.(Quran 35:2)

As a part of God's infinite wisdom all events in nature and in human life, in hardship and in ease, have a purpose and meaning. A Muslim believes in the divine decree, Pre-destination. In Arabic this is known as Qadaa and Qadar, which refer to the timeless knowledge of Allah, what He ordains and His plan. Islam is not a fatalistic religion where a person surrenders to fate or destiny without making a sincere effort. Islam teaches the human being to do their best and then leave the results to Allah. Belief in the divine decree shows the total trust of a Muslim in an All-Wise, Most-Merciful God.

The Five Pillars Of Islam

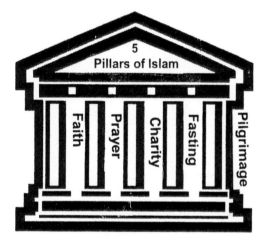

The narration about the Prophet Muhammad summarized the five pillars of Islam. They are elaborated upon here:

The 'Five Pillars' of Islam are the foundation of Muslim life:

1. **Faith or belief in the Oneness of God and the finality of the prophethood of Muhammad**
2. **Establishment of the five daily prayers**
3. **Charity for the needy**
4. **Self-purification through fasting**
5. **The pilgrimage to Mecca for those who are able**

1. Faith or Iman

ASH HADUAN LA ILA HA IL
ALLAH
WA ASH HADUANA MUHAMMAD
RASUL ALLAH
I WITNESS THAT THERE IS NO GOD BUT
ALLAH AND WITNESS THAT MUHAMMAD
(PBUH) IS THE MESSENGER OF
ALLAH

SUBMISSION TO ISLAM

The declaration of faith is called the Shahadah, a simple statement that all the faithful pronounce. "There is none worthy of worship except God and Muhammad is the Messenger of God." The significance of this declaration is the belief that the only purpose of life is to serve and obey God, and this is achieved through the teachings and practices of the Last Prophet, Muhammad.

The Shahadah is recited into the ears of each child born in a Muslim family. Others who later in their life chose the religion of Islam make the same declaration, that "there is no God but God and Muhammad is his Messenger." This means a rejection of all other deities except the one and only God whose Arabic name is Allah. The same one God of all humanity, including that of the Christians and Jews. The emphasis is that God is one and there is none like Him and a Muslim is one who submits to God. The second half of the Shahadah declares that Prophet Muhammad is the seal of Prophet-hood and implies the acceptance of all Prophets who came before Muhammad, peace be upon them all.

2. Prayer

Salah is the name of the obligatory prayers that are performed five times a day, as a direct link between the worshipper and God. There is no hierarchical authority in Islam and there are no priests. Muslims are encouraged to pray together in congregation and if possible in a mosque. Prayers are led by a learned person who knows the Quran and is generally chosen by the congregation.

Prayers are said at dawn (Fajr), mid-day (Zuhr), late-afternoon

(Asr), sunset (Maghrib) and nightfall (Isha), and thus determine the pattern of the entire day.

Prayer Time

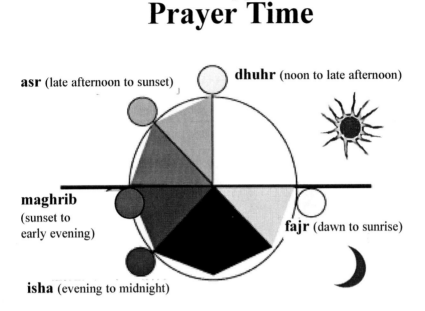

asr (late afternoon to sunset)

dhuhr (noon to late afternoon)

maghrib
(sunset to
early evening)

fajr (dawn to sunrise)

isha (evening to midnight)

These five prescribed prayers contain verses from the Quran, and are said in Arabic, the language of the Revelation. Although it is preferable to worship together in a mosque, a Muslim may pray almost anywhere, in offices, factories, or universities, as long as the place is clean. Often times strangers to the Muslim world are struck by the centrality of prayers in daily life. In the US and Europe there are many mosques and many Muslims attend "neighborhood" mosques for the dawn and evening prayers during the work-week. Sometimes at the mosque, after the dawn and evening prayers, there is a short education session where some verses of the Quran may be explained or a narration of the Prophet Muhammad is given. Listening to the Quran, understanding its message and hearing the examples of the Prophet Muhammad inspire the Muslim.

Call to Prayer

(First in Arabic then in English) Allahu Akbar Allahu Akbar

| Starting | Standing | Bowing | Sitting | Prostrating |

(God is great God is great). Ashhadu Allah ilaaha il-lal Lah (I testify that there is none worthy of worship except God.) Ash Hadu anna Muhamadar rasuulullah (I testify that Muhammad is the messenger of God.) Hayya' alas Salaah (Come to prayer.) Hayya' alal Falaah (Come to success.) Allahu Akbar (God is great) Laa ilaaha illa-Lah (There is none worthy of worship except God.)

Each declaration (except the last) is repeated twice

Note: In a non-mosque setting, such as, in the workplace or an airport, Muslims typically do not call the Azan to avoid disturbing passers by.

Summary of the prayer.

1. Intention: Person makes an intention that they are going to pray and starts by saying "Allahu Akbar" (God is Great.) 2. Quran Recitation. 3. Bowing Recite "Glory to God, the most Magnificent" 4. Sitting (between and after prostration) Recitation of more supplications 5. Prostrating Recite "Glory to God, the most High" and 6) Ends by saying "Peace and blessings of God be upon you." by facing to right and left (not shown).

Five Positions of Prayer:

3. Charity/Alms Giving

An important principle of Islam is that everything belongs to God, and that wealth is therefore held by human beings in trust. The word Zakah means "purification." Our possessions are purified by setting aside a proportion for those in need and for society in general. Each Muslim calculates his or her own Zakah individually. This involves the annual payment of a fortieth (2.5%) of one's capital/savings, excluding such items as primary residence and car. This means taking stock of all savings and giving to the needy, starting with relatives, then the community and then at an international level.

Zakah is similar to fasting as it teaches empathy with those who have little. Living in America and Europe we are blessed with every kind of food to eat, clothes to wear, and a safe warm house. Sadly for much of the world's population this is not the case. Zakat brings balance and equity in the world. Although Zakat can be paid any time during the year many Muslims prefer to give it in the month of Ramadan, because it is a blessed month.

An individual may also give as much as he or she pleases as sadaqa (optional charity) throughout the year, and does so preferably in secret throughout the year. This sadaqa, "voluntary charity" actually has a wider meaning.

The Prophet said, "Even meeting your brother with a cheerful face is an act of charity." The Prophet also said: "Charity is a necessity for every Muslim." He was asked: "What if a person has nothing?" The Prophet replied: "He should work with his own hands for his benefit and then give something out of such earnings in charity." The Companions of the Prophet asked: "What if he is not able to work?" The Prophet said: "He should help the poor and needy." The Companions further asked: "What if he cannot do even that?" The Prophet said: "He should urge others to do good." The Companions said: "What if he lacks that also?" The Prophet said: "He should check himself from doing evil. That is also an act of charity."

4. Fasting

Every year in the month of Ramadan, Muslims fast from dawn until sundown—abstaining from food, drink, and sexual relations with their spouses.

Those who are sick, elderly, or on a journey, and women who are menstruating, pregnant or nursing, are not required to fast and may make up an equal number of days later in the year if they are healthy and able. Children begin to fast (and to observe prayers) from puberty, although many start earlier.

Although fasting is beneficial to health, it is mainly a practice of self-purification and self-restraint. By cutting oneself from worldly comforts, even for a short time, a fasting person focuses on his or her purpose in life by constantly being aware of the presence of God. The Islamic calendar is based on the lunar calendar, and because of this the month of Ramadan shifts approximately 11 days each year. Ramadan is a time for spiritual rejuvenation, abstaining from the mundane and material to reflect and focus on the spiritual.

God states in the Quran:

"O you who believe! Fasting is prescribed for you as it was prescribed to those before you that you may learn self-restraint." (Quran 2:183)

5. Pilgrimage

The pilgrimage to Mecca (the hajj) is an obligation for those who are physically, financially, and mentally able to do so. Over two million people go to Mecca each year from every corner of the globe, but all with a common faith and belief to perform this rite. The Kabah (shown above) is the cube shaped building in Mecca towards which Muslims pray

The annual hajj begins in the twelfth month of the Islamic year (which is lunar, not solar). Pilgrims wear special clothes, simple garments that strip away distinctions of class and culture, so that all stand equal before God.

The rites of the Hajj, which are of Abrahamic origin, include going around the Kabah seven times, and going seven times between the hills of Safa and Marwa as did Hagar (Abraham's wife) during her search for water. The pilgrims later stand together on the wide plains of Arafat (a large expanse of desert outside Mecca) and join in prayer for God's forgiveness, in what is often thought as a preview of the Day of Judgment.

Pebbles are thrown at pillars which represent the Devil (Shaytan.) The end of Hajj is marked by a festival, Eid al-Adha, which is celebrated with prayers and the exchange of gifts in Muslim communities everywhere by people who did not go on hajj.

If Muslims and those of other faiths can comprehend the true meaning of this rite of hajj, this true peace that we all aspire to, then truly we have the opportunity to live, to co-exist in the brotherhood of Man. Malcolm X gave a narrative of the hajj experience in "Letter from Mecca' in his autobiography.

The Mosque (Masjid)

The mosque, or masjid (which means place of prostration), is where Muslims gather to pray, and is the center of many Muslim activities, including education. The first masjid, or house of worship, was built in Mecca by Prophets Abraham and Ishmaeel, and the second was built in Jerusalem forty years later. The first masjid built by the Prophet Muhammad was a very simple struc-

ture whose roof was made with date-palm leaves.

When Muslims pray they face the direction of the Holy Kabah, which is the black cube shaped building in Mecca. A small arch called the mihrab, where the Imam leads the prayers, usually identifies the direction of the Kabah. As there are no objects of worship in Islam, so there are no pictures or statues of humans or any living creation. Masjids often have important verses from the Quran engraved in the walls as well as abstract patterns. The architecture of masjids vary. Most masjids have domes and minarets, although this is not required. Did you know there are more than 2000 mosques in North America? Mosques in America and Europe are often former office buildings, schools, or churches. Some mosques also incorporate schools for both elementary and higher learning. Madarsah's are schools usually dedicated to teaching and memorization of the Quran.

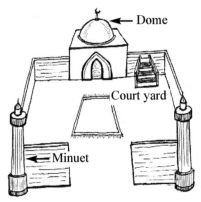

All masjids have some area where people can perform the ritual washing called wudu (ablution), where the believer washes one's hands, face, arms, head and feet to purify oneself before beginning the prayer.

The prayer area is an open area which is usually covered with prayer mats or a carpet. People take their shoes off at the door of the mosque to maintain the cleanliness of the prayer area. The prayer areas for men and women are usually separate, since the prayer is very physical, consisting of standing, bowing, and prostrating one's forehead on the ground.

The three most sacred masjids are the Kabah in Mecca, the Prophet's mosque in Medina (shown above), and the Masjid Al-Aqsa in Jerusalem. There are many other magnificent mosques in Istanbul, Cairo, Lahore, and other parts of the Muslim world. In the United States the oldest standing masjid was built in Cedar Rapids, Iowa. In London the most prominent is the Regent's Park mosque. As long as the etiquette of dressing and behaving modestly are followed, Muslims welcome people of other faiths to visit their mosques and observe the prayers. Sometimes mosques hold "open houses." Local mosques can be found by looking in the phone-book (white pages) under "Masjid" or "Islamic Center…" as well as on the Internet. Call and visit a local mosque; it is another opportunity to learn about the faith and culture of Muslims.

Muslim Festivals

There are two primary festivals that Muslims celebrate, both called 'Eid' in Arabic. The first is "Eid-ul-Fitr" which marks the end of the month of fasting, Ramadan. As Ramadan is the ninth month Eid-ul-Fitr falls on the first day of the tenth month (Shawal) in the Islamic calendar.

Muslims start the Eid day by bathing and putting on new clothes. They pay a charity before the Eid prayer called Zakat-ul-Fitr, which is money distributed to the poor so that they too can enjoy this day of happiness. The amount given is equal to the cost of a meal and should be given by each family member.

The Eid prayer may be held at the local Masjid, or if there is a large crowd may be held in places like convention centers, parks and county fair-grounds. The Eid prayer consists of a prayer and sermon that is performed after sunrise and before the noon prayer. Afterwards families and friends meet old friends. Adults pass out gifts to children, and families offer their guests confectionary. The common Eid greeting is "Eid Mubarak" which can be interpreted as "Eid greetings", congratulations and blessings

The second Eid is "Eid-ul-Adha" which takes place on the tenth day of the 12th month of the Islamic calendar called Dhul-Hajj. This is the month in which the pilgrimage or Hajj takes place. While the pilgrims are in Mecca performing the rites of Hajj, the rest of the Muslim world celebrates the "Feast of the Sacrifice," which commemorates the willingness of Abraham to sacrifice his son Ismail. Muslims believe this was a test from Allah, and that both father and son passed the test. Allah replaced Ismail with a ram.

Muslims commemorate this event by sacrificing an animal, most often a lamb or sheep, after the prayer. The sacrifice is symbolic of giving up something you love for Allah, and so the animal is slaughtered by Allah's permission. The slaughtering of the animal, called "udhiya" or "qurbani," requires selecting a healthy animal and then sacrificing it. A sharp knife must be used so as to avoid pain, and then allowing the blood of the animal to be completely drained. The meat is then divided in three, with one third given to the poor, one third for friends, and one third for the family. Due to the large number of animals that are slaughtered at Hajj time, the meat is now processed and sent to poor countries. Although it is preferable to perform the sacrifice in person, many

Muslims send their money to Islamic charities so that people in poor or deprived regions of the world can benefit.

The Two branches of Islam

After the death of the Prophet of Muhammad, a new leader had to be elected by the Muslims. After some debate the companions of the Prophet selected Abu Bakr as the first caliph (Khalifah). The caliph was both the political and religious leader.

After the death of Abu Bakr the caliphate was assumed by Omar, then Usman, and finally Ali the cousin and son-in-law of the Prophet. These four caliphs were chosen based on their righteousness and capability and are known in Muslim history as the rightly guided caliphs. When Usman the third caliph was assassinated, Ali became the caliph. Some Muslims accused Ali of being lax in bringing Usman's killers to justice. Related to this event, others challenged his authority, led by Muawia who was from the powerful Umayyad family. Muawia and his supporters position was that leadership of the Muslims should be based on ability and should not stay in the Prophet's family, implying that Ali should not be the caliph. This led to bitter conflict and resulted in supporters of Ali's family splitting off into a separate group. Ali was assassinated and his son Hussain tried to get the caliphate back, only to be killed in battle as a martyr.

Those who supported Ali and Hussain and believed this leadership should remain in the family of the Prophet became known as Shia Muslim. Those who accepted the authority of the four guided caliphs and recognized the Muslim communities right to chose its own leader became known as "Ahl al-Sunnah wa al-Jama" or Sunnis.

Shias believe there are 12 imams who were given special power by Allah, the first of whom was Ali, and from there the power was passed on through his son until the last imam, who disappeared. Shias believe he will return one day as the Mahdi. Until then the teachings are in the hands of important imams called Ayatollahs. One very famous contemporary Ayatollah was the Ayatollah Khomeni who helped bring about the Iranian revolution in 1979.

85 to 90 percent of the Muslim world population is Sunni, with the remaining being Shias. The largest population of Shias is in Iran and Southern Iraq, followed by a smaller presence in other middle east and far east countries.

It is important to note that both Shias and Sunnis believe in Allah and the Prophet Muhammad and follow the Quran. Fundamentally, they are almost the same. The difference is a political one, and lies in who are the inheritors and leaders of the Muslims after the Prophet Muhammad. The Sunnis recognize the four righteous caliphs, whereas the Shias only recognize Ali and his sons. They also have some differences of opinion about the interpretation of some parts of the Quran.

Economic and Political System of Life

As Islam is a complete way of life, Muslims have, through the example of the Prophet Muhammad and his Companions, a model of how a state should be run including the social, economical, military and political.

From an economic standpoint, at the most basic level we have to earn wealth and spend it to sustain living for us and our families. In Islam both the source must be lawful as well as where the money is spent. Beyond the needs of the immediate family come the obligation to spend on relatives and fulfill the rights of others in the community, including neighbors. The economic principles are therefore based on establishing a just and equitable society. Some of the key economic principles in Islam are:

1. The source of earnings must be lawful and permissible (Halal). Anything immoral, including earnings from gambling, usury (interest transactions), lotteries, money earned by deceit, theft, the sale and distribution of alcohol, prostitution, hoarding and any other practice which is harmful to society is unlawful. Similarly extravagance and miserliness are frowned upon.

2. The Poor tax (Zakah) establishes welfare for the less fortunate members of society. Zakah helps create equity between the rich and poor so that wealth is distributed across society.

3. Prohibition of usury or interest (Riba) is a major principle of the Economic system, as it is viewed not as trade or profit but exploitation of the needy by the wealthy. Today we live in a world

where the economic system is based on interest. Whereas Zakah takes wealth from the rich to the poor, interest takes it from the poor to the rich. The laws of inheritance, which are clearly stated in the Quran, provide another means by which wealth is shared and the rights of all the dependents are fulfilled. From a political standpoint, the basic principles are:

*Sovereignty, the source of power and all laws belongs to Allah, the Creator of mankind and the human being is the Ambassador (Khalifah) on earth, so man has to do as he is commanded.

*Government by consultation (Shura). Laws should be made with consultation and participation of the people. The Quran and Sunnah form the frame work of the Islamic legislation.

*The Ruler and the government are accountable first to Allah and then to the people. A ruler by principle is the servant of the people, and both will appear before Allah and be accountable for their actions on the Day of Judgment.

*Just as in the U.S. Constitution, the Judiciary is independent of the Executive branch. This ensures justice for all, so that a ruler and government may not interfere with the system of justice.

*All citizens are equal before the law, irrespective of religion, race, sex, color or origin. Preference of one person over another is only in piety and God-Consciousness.

To summarize, the duty of an Islamic state is to promote good and forbid evil, and be responsible for the welfare of all its citizens, using the Quran and Sunnah to benefit Muslims and non-Muslims. There is no perfect Islamic state today. However, there are revivalist Islamic efforts in different countries which are trying to establish the Sharia, the Islamic Law.

Women In Islam

Did you know that Muhammad, before his prophecy, worked for a woman, that she proposed to him and he accepted, and that he was 25 years old and she was 40? That Islam gave major rights to women over 1400 years ago in the 6th century? The right to inherit, to own property, to own business, and when in disagreement with her husband to seek divorce. Did you know that a Muslim woman can vote, enter into a legal contract, and hold positions in government? That the Hijab, the covering of women, is viewed as a liberator rather than an oppressor That in a truly Islamic society women have the right and duty to obtain an education, own property, work and earn money, the right to express their opinion and be heard. A woman has the right to refuse any marriage that does not please her, the right to negotiate marriage terms of her choice and when married, the right for all her financial needs be taken care of by her husband and the rights to keep her own money.

These are important facts that are not well known by those who lack a clear understanding of Islam. What is the status of women? What are their rights? Are men and women equal? Why do Muslim women cover their bodies and hair? What is the role of polygamy in Islam? I hope you will discover from the following essays and poems on hijab, some written by Muslim women, what Islam and its beliefs mean to them.

Status of Women

Islam views men and women as equal partners in life. They have complementary roles, so one cannot be considered inferior to the other. The creator of both men and women is God, and one of God's attributes is that he is just. The Quran and the Prophet by example show that women must be treated with kindness under all circumstances. Whereas men have the traditional role and obligation of being the primary provider and protector, the domain of the home and children is the wife's. Women are free from the drudgery of work; even housework is not an obligation. Women can and do work. This verse from the Quran addresses the believing men and the believing women as equals:

"Surely the men who submit and the women who submit, and the believing men and the believing women, and the obeying men and the obeying women, and the truthful men and the truthful women, and the patient men and the patient women and the humble men and the humble women, and the almsgiving men and the almsgiving women, and the fasting men and the fasting women, and the men who guard their private parts and the women who guard, and the men who remember Allah much and the women who remember— Allah has prepared for them forgiveness and a mighty reward." (Quran 33:35)

If put into historical context Islam and the Prophet Muhammad have truly elevated the position of women. The Prophet asked people to look upon wives with love and to cherish their daughters. Their good upbringing provides a path to paradise. Wives all over the world are abused, yet the Prophet has set the standard that the best in faith is the one who behaves best to his wife. Among parents, mothers have the highest of ranks, and a person who serves his mother well can gain entry into paradise.

Women were and have been liberated through Islam. They have gained their human rights, civil rights, social rights, economic rights, and political rights. Women (just like men) are equal in humanity, accountability, in freedom of choice and expression, the right to education, to vote, to hold office, and so much more. Along with this equality is the recognition that men and women are different with unique and complimentary roles. Women have the nurturing role, men the guardian role. Women have the rights of financial support, men the obligation to provide this support.

In the case of inheritance, men often receive a greater portion of inherited wealth than woman do because men are expected to be the financial provider of the family.

Although there are dependencies between wife and husband, the wife also has an independent status, as she can earn money, own property, enter into legal contracts, and run her own business. Some of the greatest jurists, teachers, and contributors to Muslim society have been women and they are a key part of not only Muslim societies but also of any society.

Marriage

The institution of marriage in Islam is very similar to the traditional marriage in most cultures. It is the coming together of a man and woman as husband and wife as permitted by God and witnessed by the community. To address some of the misperceptions; arranged marriages are still fairly common in the Muslim world, but this a cultural practice that is changing. Either way, arranged or not, marriage cannot, by Islamic law, be imposed on a woman. The marriage contract requires that a woman willingly agrees to the marriage. Dating is not permitted but with a chaperone a couple can meet.

Polygamy

One of the most common misconceptions about Islam is that polygamy, and more specifically polygyny (the taking of more than one wife) is something Islam invented and that all Muslim men have multiple wives. The fabled "harem" is another myth that has been propagated through books and Hollywood films.

The reality is Islam did not invent polygamy, it has been practiced by mankind for thousands of years. Many of the Israelite Prophets were polygamous. Solomon (Sulaiman) is said to have had seven hundred wives and three hundred concubines, whereas

David (Dawood) is said to have ninety-nine. As recently as the Seventeenth century, polygamy was practiced and accepted by the Christian Church. The Mormons (Church of Jesus Christ of Latter Day Saints) had allowed and practiced polygamy in the United States until it was made illegal.

Islam was revealed for all societies and all times, to accommodate different social circumstances, which may warrant the taking of another wife. This right is granted, according to the Quran, only on condition that the husband is scrupulously fair. No woman can be forced into this kind of marriage if she does not wish it. A woman may make it a condition of her marriage that her husband may not take additional wives.

Polygamy is neither mandatory, nor encouraged, but merely permitted. Images of "sheikhs with harems" are not consistent with Islam, as a man is only allowed at most four wives. Furthermore he must be able to fulfill the stringent conditions of treating each wife fairly and providing for each one with separate housing. Permission to practice polygamy is not associated with mere satisfaction of passion. It is rather associated with necessity and compassion toward widows and orphans. It is the Quran that limits and places conditions on the practice of polygamy. Previously there were no constraints on the number of wives that a man could marry and wives were considered by many to be mere "property."

It is both honest and accurate to say that Islam regulated this practice, limits it, made it more humane, and instituted equal rights and status for all wives. The general rule in Islam is monogamy, and only a very small percentage of Muslims practice polygamy.

Polygamy is a solution to a specific problem; where there is an imbalance of men versus women it avoids permissiveness. Islam has an inherent flexibility and is straightforward in dealing with practical solutions to social problems. Rather than requiring hypocritical and superficial compliance, Islam delves deeper into the problems of individuals and societies. It provides for legitimate and clean solutions to problems. So the choice is not of polygamy versus monogamy, but polygamy versus sexual anarchy.

Relationship between the sexes

The word "hijab" comes from the Arabic word "hajaba" meaning to hide from view or conceal. In the present time, the context of hijab is the modest covering of a Muslim woman. Muslim women observe hijab (covering the hair and the body) because Allah commands them to. The hijab is a sign of modesty. It allows women to be evaluated for their intelligence and skills instead of their looks and sexuality. An Iranian schoolgirl is quoted as saying; "We want to stop men from treating us like sex objects, as they have always done. We want them to ignore our appearance

hijab

and to be attentive to our personalities and mind. We want them to take us seriously and treat us as equals and not just chase us around for our bodies and physical looks." Clothing of women in the early 20th century and all the way back to biblical times, shows clothing similar to hijab.

niqab

A Muslim woman who covers her hair is making a statement about her identity. Anyone who sees her will know that she is a Muslim and has a good moral character. Many Muslim women who dress modestly are filled with dignity and self esteem; they are pleased to be identified as a Muslim woman. As a chaste, modest, pure woman, who does not want her sexuality to be a factor in her interactions with men. A woman who dresses modestly is concealing her sexuality but allowing her femininity to be brought out.

Both men and women are required to dress modestly and behave with each other in a modest way by lowering their gaze. Neither should wear tight-fitting or revealing clothes. In addition women cover their bodies so that only the hands and face may be seen. The cover consists of a headscarf and loose fitting clothes. The type of dress varies based on culture, so there is much diversity. The face-veil (niqab) is more common in the Indian sub-continent, Afghanistan and Saudi Arabia. These are cultural manifestations of Islam. In Iran the veil/cover is called a chador. The Taliban enforced the wearing of the burqa for city-dwelling women, which proved to be very unpopular and seen as oppressive in the West. It is interesting that since the fall of the Taliban, most women in rural areas continue to wear the burqa.

Separation of women from men, sometimes called purdah, is practiced in most Muslim societies. In all Muslim cultures men and women pray in separate areas, just as in Jewish and other traditions. There is no generalization that can be made about how people socialize; however intermingling is not common, especially with strangers. Most women, both in cities and in villages, play an active role in the community. They are not locked in their homes, as the media often suggests.

Challenges facing Muslim women

Muslims are not immune to the influence of global culture and the environment that we live in. Marriages do break down, although not at the frequency that exists in the West. Ignorance, poverty and illiteracy are all contributing factors to the social problems that exist. As in any culture, the fall of a few does not represent overall society. Broken families and custody issues of children, including abduction, are very common in the U.S., but it is not considered a part of American culture. However, if a similar case happens to a Muslim who has an American wife it becomes not only headline news but the subject of books and movies. An example of this is the case of an Iranian husband who secretly took his daughter back to Iran. As tragic as the incident was this case was used to represent not only family life in Islam but, even more astounding as an introduction to Islam in schools via the film "Not without my daughter."

In most traditional Muslim cultures, as well as in America and Europe, it is the faith and culture which encourages women to "cover" voluntarily. The most notable exceptions, and those which have received disproportionate media coverage, are the enforcement in the past in Iran, and the Taliban regime in Afghanistan. Women have the right to education and can go to work. The ban that the Taliban enforced on women was not representative of the Muslim world at large.

However, things are changing. Of the American and British

converts to Islam more than half to four fifths are women. Of these, a greater percentage are college or university graduates. These converts, along with their second and third generation Muslim women, will hopefully help bridge the cultural gap that exists between East and West.

My body is my own business by:Ms. Naheed Mustafa

A Canadian-born Muslim woman has taken to wearing the traditional hijab scarf. It tends to make people see her as either a terrorist or a symbol of oppressed womanhood, but she finds the experience liberating.

"I often wonder whether people see me as a radical, fundamentalist Muslim terrorist. Or maybe they see me as the poster girl for oppressed womanhood everywhere. I'm not sure which it is.

I get the whole gamut of strange looks, stares, and covert glances. You see, I wear the hijab, a scarf that covers my head, neck, and throat. I do this because I am a Muslim woman who believes her body is her own private concern.

Young Muslim women are reclaiming the hijab, reinterpreting it in light of its original purpose — to give back to women ultimate control of their own bodies.

The Quran teaches us that men and women are equal, that individuals should not be judged according to gender, beauty, wealth, or privilege. The only thing that makes one person better than another is her or his character.

Nonetheless, people have a difficult time relating to me. After all, I'm young, Canadian born and raised, university-educated — why would I do this to myself, they ask.

Strangers speak to me in loud, slow English and often appear to be playing charades. They politely inquire how I like living in Canada and whether or not the cold bothers me. If I'm in the right mood, it can be very amusing.

But, why would I, a woman with all the advantages of a North American upbringing, suddenly, at 21, want to cover myself so that with the hijab and the other clothes I choose to wear, only my face and hands show? Because it gives me freedom. Women are taught from early childhood that their worth is proportional to their attractiveness. We feel compelled to pursue abstract notions of beauty; half realization that such a pursuit is futile.

When women reject this form of oppression, they face ridicule and contempt. Whether it's women who refuse to wear makeup or to shave their legs, or to expose their bodies, society, both men and women, have trouble dealing with them.

In the Western world, the hijab has come to symbolize either forced silence or radical, unconscionable militancy. Actually, it's neither. It is simply a woman's assertion that judgment of her physical person is to play no role whatsoever in social interaction.

Wearing the hijab has given me freedom from constant attention to my physical self. Because my appearance is not subjected to public scrutiny, my beauty, or perhaps lack of it, has been removed from the realm of what can legitimately be discussed.

No one knows whether my hair looks as if I just stepped out of a salon, whether or not I can pinch an inch, or even if I have unsightly stretch marks. And because no one knows, no one cares.

Feeling that one has to meet the impossible male standards of beauty is tiring and often humiliating. I should know, I spent my entire teen-age years trying to do it. I was a borderline bulimic and spent a lot of money I didn't have on potions and lotions in hopes of becoming the next Cindy Crawford.

The definition of beauty is ever changing; waifish is good, waifish is bad; athletic is good — sorry, athletic is bad. Narrow hips? Great. Narrow hips? Too bad.

Women are not going to achieve equality with the right to bare their breasts in public, as some people would like to have you believe. That would only make us party to our own objectification. True equality will be had only when women don't need to display themselves to get attention and won't need to defend their decision to keep their bodies to themselves."

A message from a hijab clad woman

What do you see when you look at me,
Do you see someone limited, or someone free?
All some people can do is just look and stare,
Simply because they can't see my hair,
Others think I am controlled and uneducated,
They think that I am limited and un-liberated,
They are so thankful that they are not me,
Because they would like to remain 'free',

Well free isn't exactly the word I would've used,
Describing women who are cheated on and abused,
They think that I do not have opinions or voice,
They think that being hooded isn't my choice,
All they can do is look at me in fear,
And in my eye there is a tear,
Not because I have been stared at or made fun of,

But because people are ignoring the One up above,
on the day of judgment they will be the fools,
Because they were too ashamed to play by their own rules,
Maybe the guys won't think I am a cutie,
But at least I am filled with more inner beauty,
See I have declined from being a guy's toy,

Because I won't let myself be controlled by a boy,
Real men are able to appreciate my mind,
And aren't busy looking at my behind,
Hooded girls are the ones really helping the Muslim cause,
The role that we play definitely deserves applause,
I will be recognized because I am smart and bright,

And because some people are inspired by my sight,
The smart ones are attracted by my tranquility,
In the back of their mind they wish they were me,
We have the strength to do what we think is right,
Even if it means putting up a life long fight,
You see we are not controlled by a mini skirt and tight shirt,
We are given only respect, and never treated like dirt,

So you see, we are the ones that are free and liberated,
We are not the ones that are sexually terrorized and violated,
We are the ones that are free and pure,
We're free of STD's that have no cure,
So when people ask you how you feel about the hood,
Just sum it up by saying 'baby its all good.'

Contemporary Issues

Post-Colonial Fever

When the European powers succeeded in conquering and occupying much of the Muslim world from the 17th to the 20th century, they also destroyed or set back a whole culture and civilization. Universities and schools were closed, and a separation of religious and secular schools was created. Religious and political leaders were killed and whole populations disenfranchised. Western-educated secular natives were brought in as rulers. The results have been disastrous.

The last of the Muslim caliphates, the Ottoman Empire, was dismantled by European Colonial powers (of England, France, Spain, Portugal, Holland, and Belgium) in 1924. After World War II, many countries began claiming and fighting for their independence. The de-colonization process dramatically increased the number of sovereign states. Approximately 150 new states have been created since then, of which 53 are Muslim.

In the twentieth century there have been two major world wars and many smaller wars and conflicts. Although we should not live in the past we must understand the root cause of these conflicts, as the holocausts of the past are the on-going genocides of today.

The colonial powers carved up the lands into many nations, often delineated by drawing arbitrary lines on a map. At times nation-states were not based on ethnicity, religion, language, or customs. In many cases these borders divided villages, towns, even families, and have had divisive and destructive effects on economic, social, and cultural life. Some-times the lines are drawn solid and others are dotted. Either way, they are artificial constructs which in many cases resulted in on-going turbulence.

The Prime Minister of England, Winston Churchill, once said, "The British never draw a line without blurring it," and so it is today that many of the repeated conflicts, for example, between India and Pakistan over Kashmir, Israel and the Arab states over Palestine, are a result of this ambiguity. Churchill also once boasted that he created Jordan one afternoon in the drawing room. So a valid question arises: should we live with the legacy of borders that were created by the whim of the colonialist powers of the past? What gives the occupier who subjugated its people the right to redistribute the land, it's resources and political power in a way that does not serve the long-term interests of the occupied? There are so many questions and so few answers.

The borders that divide the Kurdish people over several countries such as Iraq, Iran, Turkey, Armenia, and Syria, are neither natural, economic, nor cultural borders. Their land and people are divided. Like all other nations, the Kurds, Kashmiri's, and Palestinians have the right to independence and self-determination, and until that right is obtained, the line in the sand will remain the line of inequity and injustice.

The transition from colony to nation-states was done by setting up bureaucracies by the former colonial power structures that often did not suit the population of the new states. The result has been civil wars, tribal, religious and other minority group conflicts.

The only "stability" in some cases has been through authoritarian regimes. Where democracy played a minor role there have been a lack of mature and stable governments. It would, however, be unfair to put all of the blame for current problems on the colonizers. However, as this has been given very little currency and discourse when discussing present day issues, the issue is introduced here.

Many of the issues related to the Muslim world are not unique to Islam. At a higher level, these are common issues of humanity, independent of north versus south and east versus west. Many of the root causes of war lie in injustice and inequity. Injustice at the governmental level can lead to dictatorships and gross human rights violations. Governments who hold power using repressive means succeed temporarily. Whereas injustice is an inequity in power, inequity in wealth leads to poverty. It is an irony for the Muslim world that due to the break-up of the Ottoman Empire, there are new nations that have been fabricated. Some of them have the greatest wealth due to oil, and the smallest populations. Then there are nations with large population like Pakistan, Indonesia and Egypt, which are amongst the poorest.

Poverty, illiteracy, and suffering are major factors in civil and local wars and in the growing north-south, east-west tensions. Money which should be spent on food, education and housing is being diverted to military expenditures. Regardless of which type of government has developed, it is the power elites and bureaucracies that maintain power and who have ultimately benefited from the internal resources and foreign aid.

Until the prerequisites for sustainable peace are fulfilled, any society, including all Muslim lands, will remain unstable and prone to violence -- either civil conflict or external wars. Until basic human needs, both spiritual and material, are fulfilled, people will behave in irrational ways -- in ways, which we cannot understand or explain.

Until humanity, can break away from the physical and mental shackles of colonialism, neo-colonialism and re-colonialism, there will always be underlying currents of instability. Ultimately, there is a need to move beyond the past, and learn history's lessons. The torch of power has and always will be passed on by divine decree. The rise and fall of nations is a cycle that will continue. It is up to us to decide which part of the cycle we want to be a part of.

Muslim Nations: The conflict and the cure

There are many "hotspots" in the Muslim world that have been embroiled in some type of conflict for independence. Some began right after World War II and others that have come to the forefront in the last decades. Palestinians want independence from Israel, Kashmiris from India, Chechens from Russia, Sudan an end to foreign backed southern rebellion, Azerbaijan an end to Armenian occupation and the Chinese Muslims independence or autonomy in Xinjiang from China. We have witnessed the brutal genocide of the Bosnian and Kosovar Muslims from Yugoslavia. Besides the right to self-determination, Muslims are looking for the right to live according to Islamic law (Shariah) in their lands and to live their lives without interference from the east or the west.

At the most basic level, these are legitimate goals. The issue and challenge is how to achieve them in a world that views Islam as the "other." In the noise, one thing that must not be forgotten is that in each hotspot, the conflicts did not start with violence. When the world community did not take any concrete steps to help, and days turned to months, years and decades, frustration, deprivation, and desperation led to militant opposition. For example, other than the conflicts between Pakistan and India over

Kashmir, the Kashmiri Muslims did not take up arms against India until 1989.

Until the underlying injustices and oppression are addressed, and unless there is a desire by all parties to understand and empathize with the "other," that there is a desire for social justice, and acceptance of a people for their right to self determination, we all become the victims of this inequity. One of the many lessons that September 11th has taught us, is that terrorism has no bound-aries.

Muslims are looking for a redress for centuries of colonization and oppression that has been directed against them. It is this lega-cy of post-colonial fever which is leading to the turmoil in the Muslim world, and the only cure for this is a just democratic solu-tion for the people, by the people. Give the Palestinians and the Kashmiri's their lands with full autonomy. Oppression only begets violence when the threshold of human rights, dignity, and respect are taken away. Although these may be the underlying currents of these conflicts, that in no way justifies terrorism from any side.

Media Manipulations

After World War II, Jewish military groups in Palestine, including the Irgun and Stern organizations, successfully drove out the British authorities and the Palestinian people and con-tributed to the establishment in 1948 of the state of Israel. They were recognized at the time for their terrorist activities, yet many of them became prime ministers of Israel, including Menachin Begin and Ariel Sharon. Ariel Sharon was convicted of support-ing the massacres of over 2000 Palestinian refugees in Sabra and Chatilla in Lebanon. He sparked the second Palestinian Intifada by taking an army contingent to the sacred Al Aqsa mosque, resulting in the killing since then of over a thousand Palestinians. Who is the terrorist and who are the terrorized? Is it war or is it terrorism? Are they terrorists or freedom fighters? These are rhetorical labels and ultimately lie in the eye of the beholder, in the words and images of the press and in the barrels of guns. They are labels, which are used to describe violence conducted by a state versus those who feel they are fighting for some legitimate cause.

Unfortunately a minority can manipulate the majority. Especially with the means the media have they can paint war peace and peace war, this can result in painting slaughtering innocent civilians as collateral damage which seems nicer and gentler.

For the benefit of humanity, we need to come to a common understanding and definition of language and how it is used. Only then can we start to address the gross violations against human rights and the needless loss of human life and suffering that accompanies any act of violence. Language can be used by a dictator or president, friend or foe to excite prejudice and get the masses to behave in unthinkable ways. This has resulted in criminal violence bombings, murder, rape, kidnapping and hijacking. Legitimate goals for seeking statehood cannot be justified by illegitimate means; this is a fundamental principle of Islam. "All means necessary" needs to be translated to "All lawful means necessary," both in terms of religious and secular laws.

Information is power and information is wealth so whoever controls the content and distribution of information has unprecedented power and absolute power corrupts. So now there are media empires ruled by media titans. What is news and what is not, what gets high profile versus what does not lies in the grasps of the mighty media. Those who dominate the information networks control the views and news, and the interpretation of those events.

Whether it be one channel or a hundred channels, the news agencies form the spotlight for who is in the light and who is left in the dark, who is cast as the hero and who is cast as the villain. No nation, its people, or its leadership openly approve of violating human rights or subjugating its people. Yet human suffering continues throughout the world and especially in the Muslim world. The reality is Muslims face political and economic oppression.

The media magnifies the suffering of some and downplays it for others like the Palestinians or the Kashmiri people. The freedom of one nation, which is lauded, means the subjugation of another; the justice of one is injustice to another. It is not only warfare but also word-fare that can be so damning. Whereas the occupier fights in "self-defense" the occupied are the aggressors. Whereas the occupied people just "die" the occupiers are "murdered" or "killed." Whereas the occupier acts with "restraint and law and order," the occupied are "lawless". Remember wars are fought between two equals. A military force equipped with all the latest air power and heavy weaponry like tanks cannot be engaged in "war" against stone-throwing civilians acting in civil disobedience.

Freedom, progress, success, war, and other words like this have taken on a new meaning. We collectively, as humans, must come to a common understanding of what is right or wrong, good or evil and from an Islamic perspective this is by divine decree. The victim and victimizer are not the same.

With most of the mainstream media, the terms "Islamic, Muslim fundamentalist, terrorist" are used interchangeably and with Muslim prefixes. Yet when Jewish gun men kill Muslims praying in a mosque, Hindu mobs level mosques and rape and pillage Muslim communities, the IRA guerrilla sets off a bomb in an urban area, or Serbian Orthodox militiamen rape and kill innocent Muslim civilians, these acts are not used to stereotype an entire faith. Never are these acts attributed to the religion of the perpetrators.

The media works by conditioning the mind through programming and repetition. It works through cognitive dissonance by using subliminal but high-pressure sales tactics. It also works by using the Trojan Horse Theory, where by getting you to pay attention to one idea, another one is sneaked in. Most people do not believe they are that gullible, but that is exactly what the media and advertisers do, create viruses of the mind. In a large part of the coverage of the Muslim world the images and words often do not match. Muslim life is given scant value, often reduced to the rubble of collateral damage. Allah has placed a high value on life; let no one take it unjustly. The road to peace and justice is a long road, and in the era we live in, the battles that are cast are those in the minds by the media. It is up to us to look at ourselves and the world around us in an objective way.

Jihad & Struggle

Introduction

If you were driving down a road, listening to your favorite news station and you heard there had been a bombing, what would your immediate thought be as to who did it?

If your subconscious came up with the name "Muslims," then it would be no surprise. Even Muslims, when they hear this news story are saying "Oh Allah please let it not be Muslims." There are real events, including the bombings of the World Trade Center, events in the occupied territories of Palestine, and other news which condition us to a response like this. The danger is that this Pavlovian response is creating suspicion which can lead us astray. The Oklahoma city bombing is a classic case, as in the first few days after the bombing all eyes were on the Muslims. It was only after several days that the focus shifted to the real culprits, Timothy McVeigh and his accomplice.

The media has often equated Jihad with terrorism. Any random, irresponsible, senseless act of violence and terrorism is now called jihad. Jihad has been made synonymous to Islamic terrorism, "holy war", and other oxymorons. It is extremely important to understand the real meaning and context of unfamiliar language.

The Afghans tell a tale of an American who sought enlightenment in their land. When he arrived, he asked the first Afghan he saw, "Who is the most enlightened man in your land?" The Afghan who knew no English replied, "Nami fahmam" which in their language means, "I don't know what you're talking about."

The American set out looking for this fellow named Nami Fahamam. He soon came upon a funeral procession and out of curiosity asked an onlooker who it was who had died. The Afghan not knowing English replied, "Nami fahmam." Again, "I don't know what you're talking about." The American cried, "And to think, I just missed him." The moral of the story is we must understand a people before we can benefit from them.

Jihad means to struggle. There are different levels of jihad linguistically, so it has a very broad meaning. For example the struggle of "the self" to pass an exam or to look after your family can be viewed as jihad. Jihad also includes physically fighting combatants to protect the faith and the people of Islam. The word for war in Arabic is "harb" and for fighting is "qital". Terrorism on the other hand is defined as "the indiscriminate use of violence against civilian targets to effect a desired a political outcome." There are three basic differences between Jihad used in the context of fighting and terrorism so they cannot and should not be made synonymous.

1. Jihad is against combatants, whereas terrorism is against civilians.

2. Jihad is instituted to advance an objective interest defined by Allah, whereas terrorism is to advance a subjective interest that's defined by human interests.

3. Jihad is a communal action, sanctioned by a legitimate authority which has to be regulated, sanctioned, and with limits adhered to, whereas terrorism can be a random initiative undertaken by an individual or group.

Although a lot of what serves as a basis for the "jihad equals terrorism" equation is imagined and concocted, there are instances which act as fuel for this. There is an element of reality of irresponsible actions taken by a few Muslims in the name of Islam. These actions have been exploited and magnified by those who are antagonistic to Islam. Islam does not allow Muslims to hijack airplanes filled with civilian passengers. This is not sanctioned in Islam, but a few Muslims have done this.

Islam's moral compass is based on restraint and forbearance. Muslims are told by Allah that they are going to be tested with their wealth and lives, and confronted with difficult situations but they are asked to patiently persevere, and incline to peace. Islam however, does not teach unlimited restraint. So if a party tries to destroy the faith of Islam, harm its people, then Islam gives permission to repulse this threat. So fighting is allowed to defend the people against aggression and from oppressive regimes.

The following are examples from the Quran:

"Permission has been given to those who fight because they have been wronged (oppressed) and Allah is most capable of helping them. Those who have been driven from their homes unjustly. The only thing that the enemies found against them is that they said our Lord is Allah. So in the situation where there is a physical threat to the existence of Islam, Muslims have been given permission to fight"

"Fight in the way of Allah who fight you, but don't transgress" (don't initiate.) Random indiscriminate killing is not allowed.

Wars by their nature are not holy. The Prophet Muhammad, after returning from a battle, said "We have come from the smaller jihad to the greater jihad", referring to the struggle against one's desires. Jihad can be applied to an inner struggle against ones desires, a struggle for decency and goodness, a struggle against social evils, a struggle to fight injustice or to defend oneself.

Often those who either misunderstand or choose to misrepresent Islam, extract individual verses of the Quran, taking them out of context, in time, place and correct interpretation. People read the Quran but do not know its true meaning. There are verses in the Quran which if read outwardly can be interpreted to be a license to kill people. This is not what they mean! For example in a chapter called Taubah in the Quran a group of people broke a treaty with the Muslims so the Muslims were told to fight them wherever they found them. They were a specific group of people, this verse is not a generalized verse and only applies to treachery. The Quran is a holistic body of guidance. If some people take parts of the Quran without understanding the holistic message they will go astray.

A few of the many myths include the claim that Islam was spread by the sword, that Muslims are violent, are extremists, and that Muslims, including children, are brought up to be terrorists and would-be suicide bombers.

Quite the contrary, Islam by definition cannot be forced on anyone. The Quran says "Let there be no compulsion in religion." Taking up arms is the last resort in Jihad, and is subject to rigorous conditions laid down by sacred law. Like Christianity and other faiths, Islam permits fighting to defend oneself or one's family, to fight persecution and defend those who are helpless and oppressed, in defense of religion and religious freedom, on the part of those who have been expelled forcibly from their homes, or to defend and expel tyrants. If a Muslim is killed in Jihad, that person is a martyr. How Muslims view martyrdom and fighting in a just war is no different than how Christians or people of other faiths consider their just wars and their martyrs and heroes who are slain.

Example verses from the Quran which show these guidelines are:

"And fight them until persecution is no more, and religion is for God.

But if they desist, then let there be no hostility except against wrongdoers" (2:193)

"If they seek peace, then you seek peace. And trust in God for He is the One that hears and knows all things" (8:61).

Islam gives respect and freedom of religion to all faiths. It is a function of Islamic law to protect the privileged status of minorities, and this is why non-Muslim places of worship have flourished all over the Islamic world. The life and property of all citizens in an Islamic state are considered sacred whether the person is Muslim or not.

Islam lays down strict rules of combat that include prohibitions against harming civilians and against destroying crops, trees and livestock. As Muslims see it, injustice would be triumphant in the world if good people were not prepared to risk their lives in a righteous cause. Jihad and terrorism are two distinct entities: one good, the other evil, one encouraged the other forbidden, one almost invisible and the other sloganized. Although the term Jihad is now used routinely, it is a good reminder for all that war cannot be arbitrarily waged, other than by a state and it's rightful leader.

The following chapter, describes the influence of the media and how we perceive things. It then describes some of the major issues that Muslims have faced and continue to face due to the ravages of colonialism. I call it Post-Colonial fever. Ultimately no one is opposed to real peace, freedom, democracy and the key values we uphold. The issue as I present it is how these issues are packaged and presented in foreign policy, laws and the media. The net result is that a greater part of the Muslim world is in turmoil. Some of the hotspots such as Palestine and Kashmir are discussed. The common denominator for all of them is the struggle for human rights and the right to self-determination. This chapter then leads into bridge-building.

Peace: The Greater Jihad
by Yahya

Everywhere I look and hear, there's that word jihad,
The way it's tossed around would make the Prophet sad.
When are we all going to learn what God really meant,
It's not about other people, it's destroying your own evil bent.
The greater jihad, it's not killing people.
The greater jihad, it's about fighting evil.
The greater jihad, it's a battle that's inside you.
Now that you know, what are you gonna do?

Muhammad said that the struggle in battle--that's the lesser fight,
So he fought the greater one first, so his words could be a light.
Take the plank out of your own eye, before your brother's speck,
Maybe you would stop to think--wouldn't be so quick to correct.

The war against the Soviet Union, now that was a real jihad,
But the way the "students" treat the Afghans must make God real mad.
Why did we leave the freedom fighters once they won the war,
We got what we wanted, and now we're coming back for more.

The greater jihad, it's not killing people.
The greater jihad, it's about fighting evil.
The greater jihad, it's a battle that's inside you.
Now that you know, what are you gonna do?

I know that I'm fighting my own jihad every single day,
Satan's whispering in my ear for me to come out and play.
But it's my choice, my free will, the gift that God gave me,
Choosing the harder right over the easier wrong, that will surely save me.
Man's been asking the question all along, does God create evil?

He didn't have to create it--he just created people.
Everything that's good in life comes from God's merciful hand,
And everything that's evil is done by the hand of man.

The greater jihad, it's not killing people,
The greater jihad, it's about fighting evil.
The greater jihad, it's a battle that's inside you.
Now that you know, what are you gonna do?

It's time to get up, stand up, stand up for your rights,
And sometimes that means that you have to join the fight.
But God taught man by the pen what he knew not,
It's time to speak up and write down without firing a shot.
But I say killing the evil inside each of us is the real revolution.
So let's all come together and join in our Creator's perfect plan,
Working hard to love one another and spreading peace throughout the land.

The greater jihad, it's not killing people
The greater jihad, it's about fighting evil.
The greater jihad, it's a battle that's inside you.
Now that you heard, don't say I didn't warn you.

President George W. Bush on Islam

Remarks at Islamic Center of Washington, D.C.

THE PRESIDENT: Thank you all very much for your hospitality. We've just had a wide-ranging discussions on the matter at hand. Like the good folks standing with me, the American people were appalled and outraged at last Tuesday's attacks. And so were Muslims all across the world. Both Americans and Muslim friends and citizens, tax-paying citizens, and Muslims in nations were just appalled and could not believe what we saw on our TV screens.

These acts of violence against innocents violate the fundamental tenets of the Islamic faith. And it's important for my fellow Americans to understand that. The English translation is not as eloquent as the original Arabic, but let me quote from the Koran, itself: "In the long run, evil in the extreme will be the end of those who do evil. For that they rejected the signs of Allah and held them up to ridicule."

The face of terror is not the true faith of Islam. That's not what Islam is all about. Islam is peace. These terrorists don't represent peace. They represent evil and war. When we think of Islam we think of a faith that brings comfort to over 1.2 billion people around the world. Billions of people find comfort and solace and peace. And that's made brothers and sisters out of every race — out of every race.

America counts millions of Muslims amongst our citizens, and Muslims make an incredibly valuable contribution to our country. Muslims are doctors, lawyers, law professors, members of the military, entrepreneurs, shopkeepers, moms and dads. And they need to be treated with respect. In our anger and emotion, our fellow Americans must treat each other with respect. Women who cover their heads in this country must feel comfortable going outside their homes. Moms who wear cover must be not intimidated in America. That's not the America I know. That's not the America I value.

I've been told that some fear to leave; some don't want to go shopping for their families; some don't want to go about their ordinary daily routines because, by wearing cover, they're afraid they'll be intimidated. That should not and that will not stand in America.

Those who feel like they can intimidate our fellow citizens to take out their anger don't represent the best of America, they represent the worst of humankind, and they should be ashamed of that kind of behavior.

This is a great country. It's a great country because we share the same values of respect and dignity and human worth. And it is my honor to be meeting with leaders who feel just the same way I do. They're outraged, they're sad. They love America just as much as I do. I want to thank you all for giving me a chance to come by. And may God bless us all.

A STORIED, GLORIOUS RELIGION

By Rabbi Marc Gellman & Msgr; Thomas Hartman (A Question and Answer from the God Squad Newsday, 1/26/2002)

Q. It's tough to love your enemy. Since Sept. 11, I find myself consumed with anger toward Muslims. I know only a few are terrorists, but I keep hearing that the Quran tells Muslims to kill unbelievers. I don't know what to think about Islam, and I don't know how to control my anger. - S.B.

A. Islam is not a good religion -- it's a great religion. For 1,600 years, it has had no Inquisitions, sponsored no Crusades and had no Holocaust. In 1492, when the Jewish people were expelled from Christian Spain, they were warmly accepted in Muslim Turkey. The Muslim King Hassan of Morocco, who was allied with Hitler and Mussolini during World War II, refused Hitler's orders to transport even a single Moroccan Jew to Europe for extermination. Islamic translators and philosophers, called mutikalimun, translated Plato, Aristotle and the Greek classics into Arabic when Europe was in the Dark Ages In view of this glorious past, it's particularly tragic that today Islam has been hijacked just like those planes on Sept. 11. A small number of fanatics have used Islam to justify their political agenda and their murderous obsessions. Islam also teaches that both Moses and Jesus were holy prophets from God. Jews and Christians are not unbelievers (kafirs), according to explicit Muslim teaching. In fact, the clear teaching of Islam is that "to kill one single innocent person is like killing the whole world." Islam teaches that jihad, which means struggle, justifies holy war only as a defense of one's homeland (very much like the "just war" teaching of Christianity and Judaism). It forbids killing innocent noncombatants and never allows people who are not respected Muslim scholars to issue fatwas, or religious orders. Osama bin Laden is not a scholar. His version of fatwas, his terrorism and his teachings are against every tenet of Muslim law. So condemning all of Islam for the Sept. 11 attacks is like condemning all of Christianity for the Crusades or the Inquisition. Sometimes, religions go through a time of trial and testing, and need a reformation to return to their true teachings of love and compassion. Islam seems to be going through such a time now, and we must hear the voices of those Muslims speaking out against this perversion of a great religion and pray for their ability to reclaim their faith. We non-Muslims must keep hatred out of our hearts and guard against making all Muslims scapegoats for the hateful distortions of a few maniacs.

Over One Billion people Hijacked

For most of us Americans and for a great number of citizens of the world we may clearly remember where we were on the morning of September 11th, 2001. It is a day, which has cast a permanent shadow not only in the landscape of New York but more in our hearts and minds. Not only were four planes with their passengers and crew hijacked, not only were the occupants in the World Trade Center and Pentagon hijacked, but so were the brave fire-fighters who went to rescue them. With the approximately 3000 people who lost their lives another 1.2 billion people's faith was also hijacked. There is no one who is under more scrutiny than the Muslim. Only God has the power to heal the wounds of all those who lost their loved ones.

Unfortunately a deadly mix of, propaganda injustice and distrust fuel extreme behavior in every culture. It is important that we not encourage those among us who are misguided by their fears to lash out against any people. Misunderstanding is a curable ailment, and education is its remedy.

America's Enemy

by Claire Britton-Warren

Since the terrible atrocity of Sept. 11, the beliefs and practices of Islam and Muslims — those of us who follow the path of Islam — have been under intense scrutiny. And rightly so. As Americans, we need to understand who our enemy is and, even more important, who our enemy is not. Much of the media's focus has been on the religious beliefs of the terrorists. Sadly, the terrorist groups have used their religious beliefs in an attempt to justify their actions. They have actually committed a terrible crime against the Muslim community. Not only were many Muslims killed in the World Trade Center, but also many people were misled about Islam. The actions of the terrorists were no more supported by Muslims than were the actions of Timothy McVeigh supported by Christians. Acts of terrorism are against the teachings of Islam as they are in Christianity. Islam, Judaism and Christianity are founded upon the same principles. We all worship the same God and we share many of the same prophets, such as Adam, Abraham, Noah and Jesus. Why then do we hear such horrific stories coming out of the Middle East about Muslims? We could also ask why we hear such terrible stories about corruption in the Christian clergy. The acts of individuals should not be judged as reflecting the beliefs of their religious communities.

In every religious group, it is important to understand the values of the mainstream. Of the 1.2 billion plus Muslims worldwide, the mainstream has given the media very little to talk about. We're generally a well-behaved bunch who don't drink or cheat on our spouses. We live quietly and, by praying five times a day, we involve God in our daily lives. Cultural traditions of Muslim countries can confuse those trying to understand Islam. Some cultural and national traditions actually contradict Islamic teachings.

A good rule of thumb is that if something suggests that it is acceptable to hurt or oppress anyone, or suggests intolerance of the beliefs of others, it is probably culturally based rather than Islamic.

Some aspects of Islam may appear extreme by Western standards. A Muslim woman's style of dress seems symbolic of oppression and subservience to men, when in fact it is merely a modest outfit which allows her to be recognized as a Muslim woman. In a culture that understands Islam, she is viewed as a religious and virtuous person who should not be annoyed with whistles and catcalls. In fact, Muslim women have all the rights of women in America as well as a few rights that American women do not have. A Muslim woman can work; own her own business and own property separately from her husband. She can earn her own income and can spend it however she pleases. Muslim women are not required to use their incomes to support their families, as that is the sole responsibility of their husbands.

My American Jihad

by Zayed Yasin

Zayed Yasin delivered this speech at Harvard University's commencement ceremony on June 6th. Its original title, "My American Jihad," sparked a protest from students angry that the speech did not condemn the terrorist attacks of September 11. The title was changed to "Of Faith and Citizenship: My American Jihad," but Mr. Yasin did not change the content of his speech.

"I am one of you. But I am also one of "them." What do I mean? When I am told that this is a world at war, a war between the great civilizations and religions of the earth, I don't know whether to laugh or cry. "What about me?" I ask. As a practicing Muslim and a registered voter in the Commonwealth of Massachusetts, am I, through the combination of my faith and my citizenship, an inherent contradiction?

I think not. Both the Quran and the Constitution teach ideals of peace, justice and compassion, ideals that command my love, and my belief. Each of these texts, one the heart of my religion, the

79

other that of my country, demand a constant struggle to do what is right.

I choose the word "struggle" very deliberately, for its connotations of turmoil and tribulation, both internal and external. The word for struggle in Arabic, in the language of my faith, is jihad. It is a word that has been corrupted and misinterpreted, both by those who do and do not claim to be Muslims, and we saw last fall, to our great national and personal loss, the results of this corruption. Jihad, in its truest and purest form, the form to which all Muslims aspire, is the determination to do right, to do justice even against your own interests. It is an individual struggle for personal moral behavior. Especially today, it is a struggle that exists on many levels: self-purification and awareness, public service, and social justice. On a global scale, it is a struggle involving people of all ages, colors, and creeds, for control of the big decisions: not only who controls what piece of land, but more importantly who gets medicine, who can eat.

So where is our jihad, where is our struggle as we move on from Harvard's sheltering wall? Worthy adversaries are innumerable. We can turn our struggle to the war against oppression, poverty, disease...But before looking outward, we must first look inward. Before deciding what we are against, we must decide what we are for. The only way to define the inner moral force that drives our struggle is to learn through action—to get our hands dirty. To strive to see the world as it sees itself, testing the boundaries of what we think we know, and how we know it. To combine our academic search for truth with a sense of empathy for our fellow humanity—to seek Veritas in Humanitas.

On one level it's simple: everyone wants the same things that we do. The true American Dream is a universal dream, and it is more than a set of materialistic aspirations. It is the power and opportunity to shape one's own life to house and feed a family with security and dignity, and to practice your faith in peace. This is our American Jihad.

As a Muslim, and as an American, I am commanded to stand up for the protection of life and liberty, to serve the poor and the weak, to celebrate the diversity of humankind. There is no contradiction. Not for me, and not for anyone, of any combination of faith, culture and nationality, who believes in a community of the human spirit.

Some of this is a mantra that has been spoken at myriad graduations. Worth repeating, perhaps, but nothing new. What is new was taught us by last fall's tragedy and carnage. The status quo is shattered, and we have now been forced to engage more closely the troubles of this world. We are in a privileged position to shape a more just, peaceful, and honorable global society.

So I ask again: where is our jihad? Whether on our way to an investment bank in New York, or to Sierra Leone to work with orphans, Harvard graduates have a responsibility to leave their mark on the world. So let us struggle, and let us make our mark. And I hope and pray that our children, our grandchildren, and those who take our seats in the years to come, will have cause to be proud."

Muslims against Terrorism
(Quotes & Statements regarding September 11)

"By God, he is not a true believer, from whose mischief his neighbors do not feel secure." Prophet Muhammad

"Hurt no one so that no one may hurt you. Remember that you will indeed meet your Lord, and that He will indeed reckon your deeds." From the last sermon of Prophet Muhammad.

"Whoever does good equal to the weight of an atom shall see it...and whoever does evil equal to the weight of an atom shall see it." (Quran 99:7-8)

The following statements by high ranking international Muslim scholars and leaders appeared in an advertisement placed by the Becket Fund for Religious Liberty, in the New York Times, October 17th, 2001

"Hijacking Planes, terrorizing innocent people and shedding blood constitute a form of injustice that can not be tolerated by

Islam, which views them as gross crimes and sinful acts." Shaykh Abdul Aziz al-Ashaikh, Grand Mufti of Saudi Arabia and Chairman of the Senior Ulama, on September 15th, 2001

"The terrorists acts, from the perspective of Islamic law, constitute the crime of hirabah (waging war against society)." September 27, 2001 -- Fatwa, signed by: Shaykh Yusuf al-Qaradawi & other main scholars of Islam

"Neither the law of Islam nor its ethical system justify such a crime." Zaki Badawi, Principal of the Muslim College in London. Cited in Arab News

"It is wrong to kill innocent people. It is also wrong to praise those who kill innocent people." Mufti Nizamuddin Shamzai, Pakistan. Cited in the New York Times, September 28, 2001.

"What these people stand for is completely against all the principles that Arab Muslims believe in." King Abdullah II, of Jordan; cited in the Middle East Times, September 28, 2001.

"Those terrorists must be reading a completely different Quran than the rest of us. This isn't about Islam. It's about terrorism." US Marine Corps Captain Aisha Bakkar-Poe.

"Terrorists claiming to act in the name of Islam is like a knife through my heart - that people would practice Islam, but do deeds like what they've done. It's not true faith. Some people twist religion to the way they think." US Army Captain Arneshuia Balial, a convert to Islam since 1987.

Quotes by Muhammad Ali on 9-11

* "Rivers, ponds, lakes and streams — they all have different names, but they all contain water. Just as religions do — they all contain truths."

* "I'm a Muslim. I've been a Muslim for 20 years. . . . You know me. I'm a boxer. I've been called the greatest. People recognize me for being a boxer and a man of truth. I wouldn't be here

representing Islam if it were terrorist."

* I think all people should know the truth, come to recognize the truth. Islam is peace." Ali speaking on September 21, 2001 at a fundraiser for victims of the WTC and Pentagon attacks "Prejudice comes from being in the dark; sunlight disinfects it."

* "Hating people because of their color is wrong. And it does-n't matter which color does the hating. It's just plain wrong."

* "It's lack of faith that makes people afraid of meeting chal-lenges, and I believed in myself."

* "Service to others is the rent you pay for your room here on earth."

* "I wish people would love everybody else the way they love me. It would be a better world." (from Healing, a Journal of Tolerance and Understanding)

Love & peace Messages

Times of tribulation bring out the best and in others the worst of what mankind can offer. All praise is to God who provides goodness in all societies.The following are a sample of the mes-sages left by neighbors and co-workers of Muslims. These are exact words.

"I was listening to the news and reading the paper when I heard that you were receiving a lot of angry threats. I just wanted to send a message that I, your average American, have grown up here. I have talked with all my friends and family and we are very concerned about your community. And we have been thinking about you here and we are glad you are here. We hope that you are safe and we don't feel any anger towards the community, and we understand it was an act of individuals. And just wanted to give you our reassurance we are behind you guys."

"I'm sure you're receiving a lot of hateful calls. Most of us understand you are struck by the tragedy as we all are and there is no connection between you and people who perpetrated the crime, and we stand in solidarity with you in that way."

"I am a Japanese American and I just wanted to pledge my support to your organization, or anything I can do to help alleviate some of the discrimination you many be experiencing. I will be happy to attend any meetings or be a spokesperson on your behalf."

"I wanted to wish the Muslims' community salaam (peace). What the terrorist did didn't represent Islam and I just wanted to wish you and all the Muslim community peace and wanted to say salaam. And God be with you. Peace."

"Just wanted to let you know I support your work. I'm a Jew and very concerned about the reactions against the American Muslims and I don't want to that happen, and my heart goes out to your people."

"Not all Americans are hateful towards Muslims in general. The silent majority of Americans don't feel that way and we condemn anyone who attacks you or sends hateful phone calls."

"I hope you have not been getting many hate calls because that's the worst side we can show you. Thank you for your kind message. I am an atheist, of European decent. Just hang on."

A letter to co-workers

Dear Colleagues,

With the tragic events of last Tuesday, all of us have and are going through a state of disbelief that such an event could happen and angry at those who did such a heinous act. I asked our HR department if they would allow me to send this email as one of the many things we as a nation need to do to start the long road to healing.

First, let me say as a Muslim that this act was an act of terrorism. It had nothing to do with Islam or Muslims. Human life is the most priceless of gifts we have been given. In Islam, Allah (the Arabic word for the one and only God) impresses the value of life in the Holy Quran , "Whosoever kills an innocent life without a right, it is as the killing of all humanity. Whosoever saves a human life, it is as saving all of humanity." No one in the name of any religion could do such an act. The Prophet Muhammad even in a state of war (which is not the case here), forbade the killing of women, children and innocent civilians, from uprooting trees, burning crops and poisoning water wells.

Second, media coverage has pointed to Muslims and Arabs as the perpetrators of this crime. Because of this continual portrayal of bias in the media many hate crimes have been committed against Muslims, Arabs and those who resemble them, including Sikhs. Just as Timothy McVeigh or Jim Jones did not represent Christians, or Americans, similarly it would be a gross injustice to implicate all Muslims or Arabs using "guilt by association." Amongst others, all Muslim nations as well as American Muslim and Arab organizations have condemned this act of terrorism. This is the time for all of us to show empathy not only to those in New York, or Washington, but wherever innocent civilians are being persecuted and killed.

In conclusion, one of the pillars of this country is due process, which even Timothy McVeigh was allowed. We should not hasten to be judge, jury and executioner as this is what separates terrorists from a civilized society. Ramsey Clark, a former US Attorney General said about violence, "This is what America must do. We must strive for justice with all our might while constantly and consciously controlling our inner impulse to violence."

May God give us all the patience, wisdom, strength and resolve to do what is right.

Javed Mohammed

Co-worker responses

First Reply

Very well done. Thank you for adding a voice of peace and reason to the cacophony of hatred, fear, and ignorance that the despicable acts of a few criminal madmen has turned loose.

Unfortunately, a lot of people seem to be letting their emotions get in the way of their better judgment. President Bush has said many times over the last few days that "If America attacks, it will not be an attack on Islam," and "the Islamic faith is one of peace". Why do people forget this?

As you confirmed, the Quran forbids killing women, children, and innocent civilians. Yet these extremists, who claim to follow the Quran, killed women, children, and innocent civilians. Were these important words from the Quran in their thoughts as they piloted the airliners into their targets? Also, if their goal was to strike a blow to an intractable enemy, then why did they have to kill fellow Muslims as well? No matter how you think about it, it just does not make any sense.

What these people should realize is that anyone who truly practices their respective religion (I am a Christian myself) should bring no harm to anyone. All of the world's true religions (not cults) state that killing is the worst evil. I believe that it doesn't matter what label a person's religion has as long as that person follows the TRUE teachings of that religion: live in peace with your neighbors.

I dream of a day when all people who believe in God, whether it be Jehovah, the Christian God, Allah, the Hindu God, or Buddha, can come to love and respect each other and not pass judgment on others who do not believe in God the same way. I dream of a day when all people can come to love and respect other people whether they believe in God or not, and people do not try to push their beliefs on others. Religion should be based on true faith in God, not on brainwashing or coercion.

Terrorists are brainwashed into believing they are achieving Heaven's glory by committing these evil acts. Let's pray for their souls as well as for those of their many victims. Let's pray that even just one of them will come to see that what they are doing is not right and that someone, somewhere, somehow, will lead them to a path that will surely please God. Finally, let's pray that America will exercise caution in her response and not let her emotions get in the way of her judgment.

In closing, I leave you with the Japanese word for peace:

heiwa. Hei is used to mean "level", "flat", or "equal". "Wa" means "harmony", "joining together". This makes total sense when you think about it. After all, only when people can consider each other to be equals and when people can come together in harmony, will there ever be true peace

Second Reply

Salaam aleikum,

Thanks for your moving and beautifully written memo. I believe that some good will come from this horrible event. One, hopefully, is that most Americans will have a greater understanding of Islam, and therefore will have a greater acceptance of it (at least those Americans who are even a little open-minded should be enlightened by what they read and hear). Another, hopefully, is that the Arab community in the US, and Muslims in general, will become more cohesive and therefore increase their political influence in the US. From these two things, a lot can be accomplished...eventually (inshalla).

Follow-on: Anyway, my experience gave me great respect for Islam and for Muslims in general. (It also gave me great empathy for the plight of the Palestinians, for which the US government must also be held accountable.) I very much fear for what the US government will do. In the end, it's usually the common people who suffer.

By the way, even though I was raised as a Christian, almost every day, I say to myself the words "Insh'Allah." It seems to me to be a very humble and appropriate way to look at life.

I hope no one is giving you or your family any problems. There are stupid and ignorant people in every society, and it's times like these that they appear.

If anyone hassles you, don't forget the hot-line.

best regards

Third Reply

I have been meaning to write to you regarding your email. On behalf of many Muslims, Arabs and Middle Eastern origin people I would like to take this time and thank you for clarifying so much for so many people. Especially at this time we need for everyone to know that we are all one (Americans/United at this time) there is good and bad in everyone and every religion and cultures and nationality.

We have chosen to make this land our country and we are raising our families and planting our roots in it. We need not to forget what attracted us to come here, the freedom of speech, religion and the rest of our constitutional rights. And for this we need to make sure that it is not tarnished and it is preserved.

Thank you again from the bottom of my heart. What you said is so true, "That out of adversity comes opportunity." I am a Christian Assyrian, but I was born in Baghdad, Iraq and moved here when I was 13 years old. My dad, who was also born in Iraq, had many Arab Muslims business associates, neighbors and friends. And the loyalty and friendship that he acquired out of all the years that he lived there was unbelievable. He talked about it all the time. My aunt is married to an Arab Christian from Ramalah, Palestine.

We all need to know that people are people no matter what color, religion or ethnic background they are, there is good and evil. However everyone is entitled to be treated as a human being and to get the respect and love for one another and to live in peace on this earth. This is my feeling: in the past years (Arabs and Muslims) were stereotyped into terrorist, as wrong as it might be, but when the Oklahoma tragedy hit us we started again giving everyone the benefit of the doubt as innocent till proven guilty. But now with this I feel, as sad as it may sound, we are in the guilty till proven innocent mode, and this is not what America and we Americans are all about.

I live in community that is filled with Churches, Muslim schools and synagogues. God is everywhere no matter whose God he is. Right after the tragedy of Sept 11th, two Assyrian churches were targeted the weekend of Sept. 22-23. A note left at an

Assyrian church in Roselle asked, "Are you with U.S. or with the enemy?" And someone set a fire at St. John's Assyrian American Church, causing at least $200,000 in damage. And that is because some people were upset and wanted to retaliate and we are from the Middle East.

FAQs on 9-11 Attacks Regarding Islam and Muslims

Developed by Islamic Networks Group (ING)
Islam, Muslims, and the September 11 attacks

1) Why did they do it? What do terrorists want?

No one knows for sure what motivates people to do such an evil act. It might be in revenge for things that America did that they think are wrong. Obviously, their intent was to kill many people and disrupt life and human society. The motivation may have nothing at all to do with supposed religious commitments. According to media reports, Osama bin Laden hated America because our troops occupy Saudi Arabia and we support the state of Israel over the rights of Palestinians.

2) How can we win the war against terrorism?

The war against terrorism is a huge one for America due to both terrorist groups within our borders and those outside it. The Southern Poverty Law Center, a watchdog group that tracks organized hate & militia groups in this country (the forces behind Timothy McVeigh), says those groups number in the hundreds. They may actually be a greater threat to this country than threats from outside our borders.

Beyond such measures as greater security at airports, on airlines, and at important buildings, we should possibly consider all the probable causes and grievances of those committing terrorism. Ideas like freedom, equality, democracy, and basic human rights such as having enough food, medicine, housing, and security should be supported in all countries for all people. When people have their basic human needs met, they are less likely to be violent. Whereas when people have violence done to them, they are likely to respond with violence. Any violence, whether committed by a person, a group, or a nation should be condemned. The killing of any innocent person is wrong, no matter who does it.

3) What is the role of the Muslim world in combating terrorism?

An American-Muslim role in combating terrorism at home that is either committed by organized hate and militia groups, or groups based outside our borders should be viewed as equal to any other American. All Americans should work with the proper authorities to combat terrorism.

Governments of Muslim populated countries as well as religious leaders can help prevent terrorist groups in their countries by speaking out against terrorism and making sure that their people understand that it is against the teachings of Islam. They can also increase security measures, but without taking away more civil liberties or oppressing people, because that will backfire and make people more likely to commit violence. Unfortunately, many Muslim populated countries have non-democratic or oppressive governments which deny people their basic human rights. This leads to violence and terrorism.

4) Why do people in countries like Pakistan protest against us?

The government of Pakistan joined the US in its war on terrorism. However, some groups view the US as hypocritical in its fight against the Taliban while it ignores the killing of innocent Palestinian civilians by Israel.

5) Should I be afraid of anyone from the Middle East?

Just as you should not stereotype any group of people based on their background, race, or religion it is wrong to think of all people from the Middle East as being terrorists just because a few of them appear to have committed these terrible attacks. Remember that one-fifth of the world's population is Muslim, weigh this against a handful of criminals who did these deeds. This could be compared to asking if we should be afraid of all white young males because Timothy McVeigh was white, or afraid of Irish people because there is a form of terror going on in Ireland. It's important to remember that there are both good and bad people in all countries, all races, and all religions.

6) Is there anything in the Quran, which encourages the terrorists?

Nothing in the Quran encourages terrorism. On the contrary, the Quran and Hadith, which are the two primary sources of Islamic law, provide for systems that establish peace and harmony among people of all races, nationalities, and religions. Terrorists who base their actions on the Quran misappropriate Islam, as terrorist anti-abortionists misappropriate Christianity.

Afghanistan, the Taliban, and Osama bin Laden

7) How did the Taliban's practice of Islam compare with mainstream Islam?

The Taliban shared the same beliefs and basic practices, such as prayer, fasting, charity, etc. with the world's Muslims. The difference is that their interpretation of issues and practices relating to women, dress, occupations, recreation and other matters is more rigid than the understanding of mainstream Muslims. This interpretation is very much influenced by their culture and upbringing. The Taliban are Pashtuns, tribal people living in the mountains along the Afghan-Pakistani border. They were educated in religious schools run by teachers from areas that have a rigid interpretation of Islam.

8) Why did Muslims support/follow Osama bin Laden?

Most Muslims don't know any more about bin Laden than Americans of other faiths, but some are likely to question the claim that he is behind the terrorist attacks or any terrorist activities. Some Muslims overseas support him because they see him as standing up to America, which they regard as a superpower that is biased against and harms Muslims in Iraq, Palestine and other countries. They do not think that he had anything to do with the attacks, but rather that President Bush is just looking for someone to blame because he doesn't really know who is behind the attacks.

9) Is there a conflict between being a Muslim and being an American?

No there isn't, for either immigrant Muslims who have chosen America as their home and those born here and have families that are many generations American. The best way to determine what it really means to "be an American" is to look at the United States Constitution, which shares many principles with Islamic law. In addition, most of the Muslims in America are not of immigrant background, but are in fact indigenous. So, for them there is no "other place" to go back to; they are entirely American, and, in the spirit of the First Amendment, have chosen to follow Islam as their religion.

Islam and war

10) Is there anything in Islam that justifies or leads to suicide bombing or terrorism?

No, there isn't, nor is it part of Islamic history or tradition. Suicide is strongly prohibited in Islam because no one has the right to take away the life that God has given us except God Himself. Committing terrorist acts, which kill innocent civilians, is also prohibited, even during war, especially against women, children, old people, and religious people like monks and nuns. Even the cutting down of fruit trees is forbidden. In Islam, fighting, if it occurs, is to be between two groups of military personal, not with civilians.

11) What about the suicide bombings of groups such as Hamas, Islamic Jihad and now Al-Qaeda?

Muslims in places like Palestine, are fighting for their basic rights and for their homeland, have resorted to suicide bombings because they do not have the weapons or armies to fight the tanks and gun ships that are being used against them. This is our understanding of their justification. They justify the use of these attacks against civilians because they regard the entire state of Israel as being in a state of war with the Palestinian people, since it was taken from the original inhabitants against their will. The attacks like those, which occurred in New York and Washington, that are now believed to have been done by members of Al-Qaeda, are totally against the rules and spirit of Islam, which gives the highest value and sanctity to human life.

12) Are Martyrs guaranteed 70 virgins in Heaven?

This is not an authenticated Prophetic Tradition (Hadith). However, martyrs are promised a great reward from Allah. If one attains heaven, then God, who is our Creator, rewards us with what He knows will please us. In this life, we are motivated by what we understand; the reality in the afterlife is unimaginable to us in the present. The Quran has described heaven in ways that we can imagine and comprehend, and which will appeal to us and motivate us -- both men and women -- here on earth.

That being said, not every Muslim who dies in a battle is considered a martyr. One who dies because he merely loves to fight isn't considered a martyr. Similarly, one who dies for the sake of excessive tribal loyalty isn't considered a martyr. One who dies to be praised for his courage isn't considered a martyr. Only the one who dies to advance the cause of Islam within a well-defined legal context is considered a martyr.

13) Who can call Jihad? Can Osama bin Laden declare Jihad?

Islam places a great emphasis on order in its political philosophy. Anarchy and arbitrary acts are greatly condemned. Basic principles relating to Jihad are buttressed by these twin considerations. Allah orders the believers in the Quran: "O You who believe, Obey Allah, and obey the Messenger, and those in authority amongst you," (4:59). The commentators mention that those in authority amongst you are the legitimate political authorities and the scholars. These are the people who can rightfully call for jihad, in the order we have presented. Firstly, the legitimate political authorities can make such a call. Secondly, in their absence, those scholars who are universally recognized by the Muslims for their scholarship and piety.

As Osama bin Laden was neither a scholar nor a government leader, he lacked the authority to call for Jihad. His authority was only over the people who have chosen to follow him as the leader of their group.

Other questions

14) Does the Quran order the subjugation of all non-Muslims?

This is simply not the case. The Quran is a revelation, which served as the basis for the formation of a sophisticated civilization. Like all other civilizations, Islamic civilization has rules, which govern the interaction of the Islamic polity with other nations and identity groups. Within the Muslim state, non-Muslims are free to continue the practice of their religion. Their forceful conversion is strictly forbidden. Allah says in the Quran: "Let there be no compulsion in [accepting] religion!" (2:256)

Similarly, the Quran presents a set of teachings, which serve as the basis for a developed system of international relations. For example, Allah says in the Quran: "If your enemy inclines towards peace, then reciprocate, and trust in Allah," (8:61). Hence, we find in the Quran the basis for peaceful relations with non-Muslim nations, truces, trade, educational exchanges, and other facets of normal international life.

Islam is Peace by
Javad Ahmed

Islam is peace, Islam is ease,
Islam's not danger or disease.
Islam is love and prosperity.
Islam's not hatred or adversity.
Islam is salvation through repentance.
Islam has love for all in abundance.
Islam means no harm or affliction.
Islam implores you with affection.

Islam is neither maze nor craze.
Islam is giving Allah all praise.
Islam is acing through the race.
Islam will be on everyone's face.

Islam is worshipping only the Creator.
Islam's not mere numbers on a calculator.
Islam gives you power when you surrender.
Islam's not a terrorist or for a pretender.

Islam is patience and perseverance.
Islam eases your vengeance through tolerance.
Islam is life for all eternity.
Islam gives you respect, moreover dignity.

Islam is winning hearts through honesty
Islam is giving openly in charity
Islam makes you wholesome and trustworthy
Islam is in wealth as well as in poverty.

Islam is your shield against all evil.
Islam is for your soul's retrieval.
Islam is not fundamentalism or fanaticism.
Islam's not nationalism or racism.

Wake up, people, Islam is here.
Islam is here, so have no fear.

Bridge-Building

Building Bridges Between Islam and the West
by Prince Charles

Islamic spirituality and the decline of the West :

I start from the belief that Islamic civilization at its best, like
many of the religions of the East - Judaism, Hinduism, Jainism
and Buddhism - has an important message for the West in the way
it has retained an integrated and integral view of the sanctity of
the world around us. I feel that we in the West could be helped to
re-discover the roots of our own understanding by an appreciation
of the Islamic tradition's deep respect for the timeless traditions of
the natural order.

I believe that the process could help in the task of bringing our
two faiths closer together. It could also help us in the West to
rethink, and for the better, our practical stewardship of man and
his environment - in fields such as health-care, the natural environment and agriculture, as well as in architecture and urban plan-
ning. Modern materialism is unbalanced and increasingly damag-
ing in its long-term consequences. Yet nearly all the great religions of the world have held an integral view of the sanctity of the

world. The Christian message with, for example, its deeply mystical and symbolic doctrine of the incarnation, has been traditionally a message of the unity of the worlds of spirit and matter, and of God's manifestation in this world and in mankind.

But during the past three centuries, in the Western world at least, a dangerous division has occurred in the way we perceive the world around us. Science has tried to assume a monopoly - even a tyranny - over our understanding. Religion and science have become separated, so that now, as Wordsworth said, "Little we see in nature that is ours." Science has attempted to take over the natural world from God; it has fragmented the cosmos and relegated the sacred to a separate and secondary compartment of our understanding, divorced from practical, day to day existence.

We are only now beginning to gauge the disastrous results. We in the Western world seem to have lost a sense of the wholeness of our environment, and of our immense and inalienable responsibility to the whole of creation. This has led to an increasing failure to appreciate or understand tradition and the wisdom of our forebears, accumulated over the centuries. Indeed, tradition is positively discriminated against - as if it were some socially unacceptable disease.

In my view, a more holistic approach is needed now. Science has done the inestimable service of showing us a world much more complex than we ever imagined. But in its modern, materialist, one-dimensional form, it cannot explain everything. God is not merely the ultimate Newtonian mathematician or the mechanistic clockmaker. As science and technology have become increasingly separated from ethical, moral, and sacred considerations, so the implications of such a separation have become more somber and horrifying - as we see in genetic manipulation or in the consequences of the kind of scientific arrogance so blatant in the scandal of BSE.

I have always felt that tradition is not a man-made element in our lives, but a God-given intuition of natural rhythms, of the fundamental harmony that emerges from the union of the paradoxical opposites that exist in every aspect of nature. Tradition reflects the timeless order of the cosmos, and anchors us into an awareness of the great mysteries of the universe, so that, as Blake put it, we can see the whole universe in an atom and eternity in a moment.

That is why I believe Man is so much more than just a biological phenomenon resting on what we now seem to define as "the bottom line" of the great balance sheet of life, according to which art and culture are seen increasingly as optional extras in life.

This view is quite contrary, for example, to the outlook of the Muslim craftsman or artist, who is never concerned with display for its own sake, nor with progressing ever forward in his own ingenuity, but is content to submit a man's craft to God. That outlook reflects, I believe, the memorable passage in the Koran, "whithersoever you turn there is the face of God and God is all embracing, all knowing." While appreciating that this essential innocence has been destroyed, and destroyed everywhere, I nevertheless believe that the survival of civilized values, as we have inherited them from our ancestors, depends on the corresponding survival in our hearts of that profound sense of the sacred and the spiritual.

Traditional religions, with their integral view of the universe, can help us to rediscover the importance of the integration of the secular and the sacred. The danger of ignoring this essential aspect of our existence is not just spiritual or intellectual. It also lies at the heart of that great divide between the Islamic and Western worlds over the place of materialism in our lives. In those instances where Islam chooses to reject Western materialism, this is not, in my view, a political affectation or the result of envy or a sense of inferiority. Quite the opposite.

And the danger that the gulf between the worlds of Islam and the other Eastern religions on the one hand and the West on the other will grow ever wider and more unbridgeable is real, unless we can explore together practical ways of integrating the sacred and the secular in both our cultures in order to provide a true inspiration for the next century.

Islamic culture in its traditional form has striven to preserve this integrated, spiritual view of the world in a way we have not seen fit to do in recent generations in the West. There is much we can learn from that Islamic worldview in this respect.

There are many ways in which mutual understanding and appreciation can be built. Perhaps, for instance, we could begin by having more Muslim teachers in British schools, or by encouraging exchanges of teachers. Everywhere in the world people want to learn English. But in the West, in turn, we need to be taught by Islamic teachers how to learn with our hearts, as well as our heads. The approaching millennium may be the ideal catalyst for helping to explore and stimulate these links, and I hope we shall not ignore the opportunity this gives us to rediscover the spiritual underpinning of our entire existence.

Building Bridges

Building bridges physical or metaphorical are great challenges to mankind, yet when we persevere along with God's mercy we are able to build them.

Although I am not a civil engineer, it is fairly intuitive that the design of each bridge is very different, to accommodate the various terrains. Similarly the bridge of dialog, the bridge of understanding, and the bridge of empathy require different construction. All need a strong foundation and a willingness to build these bridges. For my part I am listing some of the work done by others, which build upon our commonalties.

If each and every individual makes their contribution we can go a long way to not only build bridges but also bring the hearts and minds of humanity to justice, peace and ultimately love. From a Muslim viewpoint, this can only happen by having good intentions, making our best efforts and submitting to the will of the one and only God.

A Christian and Muslim Prayer

This Muslim prayer "The Opening:" Al Fatiha is the first chapter in the Quran. It is an acknowledgement of God as the Lord of the Universe and is a prayer for His guidance. It is recited at the beginning of each prayer. Compare the following prayers and notice the similarities.

A Muslim Prayer

In the Name of God, the Compassionate, the Merciful

All praise be to God, Lord of the Universe. The Compassionate, the Merciful . Sovereign of the Day of Judgment. You alone we worship; and to You alone we turn for help. Guide us to the straight path; the path of those whom You have favored. Not of those who have incurred Your wrath, nor of those who have gone astray.
Ameen

A Christian Prayer

Our Father which art in heaven, Hallowed be thy name Thy kingdom come, Thy will be done in earth, As it is in heaven. Give us this day our daily bread; And forgive us our debts, As we forgive our debtors; And lead us not into temptation, But deliver us from evil. For thine is the kingdom and the power and the glory, for ever. Amen. (Matt. 6:9-13, KJV)

Mary & Jesus in the Holy Quran

How does Islam view Jesus? In short, very highly, he is recognized as a Messenger, Prophet, and Messiah along with other attributes. Jesus is one of the four major Prophets after the Prophet Abraham, the others being Moses, David, and Muhammad, may God's peace be upon them all. The Quran verifies the virgin birth of Jesus, his miracles, and the revelations he received in the form of the Gospel (known as Injeel in Arabic). The major differences in Islam is that Jesus's status is not divine, he is not a son of God, as Allah's attribute is that He is one. Secondly, the Quran refutes the Crucifixion, objecting to the claim that Jesus died on the cross, rather that he ascended to the heavens and will return close to the Day of Judgment as the Messiah. There are many references to Jesus in the Quran. Mary, (Maryam) is believed to be one of the four most righteous women that ever lived.

101

The following verses describe the miraculous birth of Jesus in the Quran in the chapter called Maryam (19 v16)

And make mention of Mary in the Scripture, when she had withdrawn from her people to a chamber looking East, And had chosen seclusion from them. Then We sent unto her Our Spirit and it assumed for her the likeness of a perfect man.

She said: Lo! I seek refuge in the Beneficent One from thee, if thou art Allah-fearing. He said: I am only a messenger of thy Lord, that I may bestow on thee a faultless son.

She said: How can I have a son when no mortal hath touched me, neither have I been unchaste?

He said: So (it will be). Thy Lord saith: It is easy for Me. And (it will be) that We may make of him a revelation for mankind and a mercy from Us, and it is a thing ordained.

And she conceived him, and she withdrew with him to a far place. And the pangs of childbirth drove her unto the trunk of the palm-tree. She said: Oh, would that I had died and had become a thing of naught, forgotten!

Then (one) cried unto her from below her, saying: Grieve not! Thy Lord hath placed a rivulet beneath thee, And shake the trunk of the palm-tree toward thee, thou wilt cause ripe dates to fall upon thee. So eat and drink and be consoled. And if you see any mortal, say: Lo! I have vowed a fast unto the Beneficent, and may not speak this day to any mortal.

Then she brought him to her own folk, carrying him. They said: O Mary! Thou hast come with an amazing thing.

Sister of Aaron! Thy father was not a wicked man nor was thy mother a harlot. Then she pointed to him. They said: How can we talk to one who is in the cradle, a young boy?

He spake: Lo! I am the slave of Allah. He hath given me the Scripture and hath appointed me a Prophet, And hath made me blessed wheresoever I may be, and hath enjoined upon me prayer and almsgiving so long as I remain alive, And (hath made me) dutiful toward her who bore me, and hath not made me arrogant, unblest. Peace on me the day I was born, and the day I die, and the day I shall be raised alive!

Such was Jesus, son of Mary: (this is) a statement of the truth concerning which they doubt. It befitteth not (the Majesty of) Allah that He should take unto Himself a son. Glory be to Him! When He decreeth a thing, He saith unto it only: Be! and it is. And lo! Allah is my Lord and your Lord. So serve Him. That is the right path.

The following are some verses which give a narrative from Jesus.

"Whereupon he (Jesus) spoke and said:

I am the servant of God. He has given me the Book and ordained me a Prophet. His blessing is upon me wherever I go and He has commanded me to be steadfast in prayer and to give alms to the poor as long as I shall live. He has exhorted me to honor my mother and has purged me of vanity and wickedness. I was blessed on the day I was born, and blessed I shall be on the day of my death, and may peace be upon me on the day when I shall be raised to life. Such was Jesus the son of Mary.: (19:30-34)

Jesus was born miraculously through the same power, which had brought Adam into being without a father: "Truly, the likeness of Jesus with God is as the likeness of Adam. He created him of dust, and then said to him, 'Be!' and he was." (3:59) During his prophetic mission Jesus performed many miracles. The Quran tells us that he said: " I have come to you with a sign from your Lord: I make for you out of clay, as it were, the figure of a bird, and breath into it and it becomes a bird by God's leave. And I heal the blind, and the lepers, and I raise the dead by God's leave." (3:49) Neither Muhammad not Jesus came to change the basic doctrine of the brief in One God brought by earlier prophets, but to confirm and renew it.

In the Quran Jesus is reported as saying that he came: "To attest the law which was before me. And to make lawful to you part of what was forbidden you; I have come to you with a sign from your Lord, so fear God and obey Me. (3:50)

The Prophet Muhammad said:

"Whoever believes there is no God but God, alone without partner, that Muhammad is His messenger, that Jesus is the servant and messenger of God, His word breathed into Mary and a spirit emanating from Him, and that Paradise and Hell are true, shall be received by God into Heaven. "(Hadith related by Bukhari).

The Church and Islam

Since the end of the First World War, a number of distinguished Christian scholars have forged lasting friendships with Muslims and have worked throughout their lives to undo the harm caused by centuries of anti-Muslim polemic. The conciliatory statements issued by the Second Vatican Council in the mid nineteen-sixties are a measure of these scholars' success at the official level.

The statement contained in the 'Declaration on the relationship of the Church to non-Christian religions' is particularly significant. It reads as follows:

Upon the Muslims too, the Church looks with esteem. 'They adore one God, living and enduring, merciful and all powerful, Maker of heaven and earth and Speaker to men. They strive to submit wholeheartedly even to His inscrutable decrees, just as did Abraham, with whom the Islamic faith is pleased to associate itself. Though they do not acknowledge Jesus as God, they revere him as a prophet. They also honor Mary, his virgin mother; at times they call on her, too, with devotion. In addition they await the day of judgment when God will give each man his due after raising him up. Consequently, they prize the moral life, and give worship to God especially through prayer, almsgiving, and fasting.

Although in the course of the centuries many quarrels and hostilities have arisen between Christians and Muslims, this most sacred synod urges all to forget the past and to strive sincerely for mutual understanding. On behalf of all mankind, let them make common cause of safeguarding and fostering social justice, moral values, peace and freedom.

The Ten Commandments

(Exodus 12: 1-17 & Deuteronomy 5: 6-21) Confirmation in the Quran (Chapter: Verse)

1.Thou shall not take any God except one.	1. There is no God God.except one God. (47:19)
2. Thou shall make no image of God.	2. There is nothing whatsoever like unto Him. (42:11)
3. Thou shall not use God's name in vain.	3. Make not God's name an excuse to your oaths. (2:224)
4. Thou shall honor thy mother and father.	4. Be kind to your parents if one or both of them attain old age in thy life, say not a word of contempt nor repel them but address them in terms of honor. (17:23)
5. Thou shall not steal.	5. But if the thief repents after his crime, and amends his conduct, Allah turneth him in forgiveness; for Allah is Oft-forgiving, Most Merciful (5:39)
6. Thou shall not lie or give false testimony.	6. They invoke a curse of God if they lie. (24:7) Hide not the testimony. (2:283)
7. Thou shall not kill.	7. If anyone has killed one person it is as if he had. killed the whole mankind.

to

(5:32)

8. Thou shall not commit adultery.	8. Do not come near it adultery is indecent deed and a way for other evils. (17:32)
9. Thou shall not covet thy neighbors wife.	9. Do good to your parents, relatives and wife or posses sions.and neighbors.(4:36) Saying of the Prophet Muhammad (P) "One of greatest sins is to have illic- it sex with your neighbors wife."
10. Thou shall keep the sab- bath holy.	10. When the call for the Friday Prayer is made, has ten to the remembrance of God and leaveoff your busi ness.

Parallel Sayings of Muhammad and Buddha

Although Prophet Muhammad and Buddha lived thousands of years apart, there are very similar parallels to the sayings attrib- uted to them. It is not that they said exactly the same things. It is rather that their distinctive and independent sayings show men with a similar mission, peace and happiness on earth.

Muhammad: Allah has given one of His followers the choice of receiving the splendor and luxury of the worldly life whatever he likes or to accept the good (of the Hereafter) which is with Allah. So he has chosen that good which is with Allah.

Buddha: They agreed among themselves, friends, here comes the recluse, Gotama, who lives luxuriously, who gives up his striving and reverted to luxury.

Muhammad: Wealth is not in vast riches but wealth is in self- contentment. The most enviable of my friends in my estimation is a believer with little property who finds pleasure in prayer, who performs the worship of his Lord well, who obeys Him in secret, who is obscure among men, who is not pointed out by people, and whose provision is bare sufficiency with which he is content.

Buddha: With the relinquishing of all thought and egotism, the enlightened one is liberated through not clinging.

Muhammad: Speaking about himself: Do not glorify me in the same manner as the Christians glorify Jesus, son of Mary, but say, "He is a slave of Allah and His Messenger.

Buddha: One is the way to gain, the other is the way to Nirvana, knowing this fact, students of the Buddha should not take pleasure in being honored, but, should practice detachment.

Muhammad: All creatures are God's children, and those dearest to God are the ones who treat His children kindly.

Buddha: Just as a mother would protect her only child at the risk of her own life, even so, cultivate a boundless heart towards all beings. Let your thoughts of boundless love pervade the whole world.

Muhammad: Feed the hungry, visit the sick, and free the captive.

Buddha: If you do not tend to one another then who is there to tend to you? Whoever would tend to me, he should tend to the sick.

Muhammad: Do not be a people without a will of your own saying: If others treat you well, we will also treat them well and if they do wrong we will do wrong; but accustom yourselves to do good if people do good and do not do wrong if they do evil.

Buddha: Consider others as yourself.

Muhammad: You must tell the truth. Truthfulness leads to right action. Right action leads to Heaven.

Buddha: One who acts on truth is happy, in this world and beyond.

Important Note: Muslims believe Muhammad is only a messenger who received his divine instructions from Allah to teach humanity.

Forgiveness and Empathy

To close this section I have selected some verses from the Quran which relate to forgiveness, and a poem I came across which touches upon empathy, a feeling where we put ourselves in the shoes of others to get an understanding of what they may be going through.

Forgiveness

" The way (to blame) is only against those who oppress men and revolt in the earth unjustly; these shall have a painful punishment. But indeed if any show patience and forgive, that would truly be an exercise of courageous will and resolution in the conduct of affairs. (Chapter 42 verse 42& 43)

Empathy: A poem by Amy Maddox

He prayed—it wasn't my religion.
He ate—it wasn't what I ate.
He spoke—it wasn't my language.
He dressed—it wasn't what I wore.
He took my hand—it wasn't the color of mine.
But when he laughed—it was
How I laughed and when he cried—it was how I cried.

Islamic Stories of the past,inspiration for the future

History is often an agreed upon myth since the writers of history are more likely to be the rich and powerful rather than advocates for the poor and powerless.

An old Indian tale tells of a boy who begins to question the fact that all the tiger stories his father tells him always have the tiger bagged in the end. Upon asking his father why the tiger never eats the hunter his father replies, "When the tiger learns to write, you will hear that story."

A good story is even better if it is true and history is full of stories. If we are to understand ourselves and others, the events and causes of the world we live in, then we cannot understand the present if we do not know the past. History is the fuel of the future and it is in this endeavor that we must look at the events of the present in their past so that we can hope for a better future. The Holy Quran includes many parables and stories which contain invaluable lessons. The whole life of the Prophet Muhammad (called his Seerah) is full of meaningful lessons as are His narrations called Hadith. Following this, Muslim history is replete with inspiration and wisdom.

There is a story about Mansur Ibn Mihran who had a very pious

109

servant. Once, by mistake, she spilled a bowl full of hot soup on him. His skin was burned and he looked at her in anguish. She was frightened but kept her cool and said:

"O teacher of good, remember Allah's saying."

He asked: "What is it?"

She replied: "And those who restrain their anger."

He said: "I am restraining it."

She said: "And remember his saying, 'those who forgive people.'"

He said: "Alright, I forgive you."

She said: "And remember Allah likes kind and beneficent people."

Mansur smiled and said: "Go. You are free."

Justice for all

There is a traditional story about Omar Ibn al-Khattab, (the second leader of the Muslims after the death of the Prophet Muhammad) who was given the keys to the city of Jerusalem.

Omar was a ruler of great justice and peace. Because of his noble qualities, he was given the beautiful name, Commander of the Faithful, and it was his rightful duty to receive the key to the Holy City which was the original qiblah, (the direction Muslims face while praying).

The armies that went before Omar had already entered Jerusalem and taken control of the city from the Christians who had ruled there since the time of Constantine, but when Omar came to take official possession of Jerusalem, he journeyed from Damascus to Jerusalem with only one camel and a guide. The caliph, being a man of great humility, had arranged with the guide that they would both take turns riding the camel. According to justice, he would ride for a while, then the servant would ride and he would walk.

Meanwhile, the entire city was awaiting Omar's impending arrival. The bishop of the Holy Sepulcher had announced, "The great Islamic leader is coming, We must greet him and pay our respects to him." And so all the people had gathered at the city gate, awaiting a grand royal procession. But no procession appeared. Instead, two people became visible on the horizon, approaching very slowly. When they finally reached the city, it was the guides turn to be riding, and so all the people mistook him for the caliph and rushed to greet him.

"Wait! I am not the caliph!" he protested and explained their arrangement to take turns riding and walking. The people, overwhelmed by this justice, praised the great caliph.

The bishop was also amazed by such justice. His heart filled with joy, and he handed the key of the city to Omar Ibn al-Khattab. The bishop then invited Omar to perform his prayers within their church. But when Omar saw the interior decorated with all the Christian symbols, he politely declined, saying, "I will pray just outside your doors."

Once he had finished, the bishop asked, "Why won't you please come into our church?"

"If I had prayed in your sanctuary," Omar explained, "my followers and those who come here in the future would take over this building and turn it into a mosque. They would destroy your place of worship. To avoid these difficulties and allow your church to continue as it is, I prayed outside." Again the bishop was amazed by his justice. "Today, because of your justice, faith, wisdom, and truth, you have received the key to the Holy City. But for how long will this remain in your hands? When will this sacred place come back into our possession?"

Omar Ibn al-Khattab then replied, "Today we have indeed taken over this place of worship. It is with the four qualities of faith, wisdom, justice, and truth that we have regained the city. As long as these four exist in Islam, as long as the Muslims have all four in their hands, they will retain the city. But when these qualities depart from Islam, this place of worship will change hands once again."

"If it happens that we must lose this place to someone else, it will be because we lack certitude in our faith. When the Muslims sell the truth and collect worldly wealth and seek worldly pleasures; when they lose good faith, good conduct, and the good behavior of modesty and reserve; when they relate to women in an immoral and unjust way; when they behave with backbiting, jealousy, and envy; when they lack unity and establish hypocrisy; when they destroy good deeds and degenerate into committing evil actions-when all this occurs in the midst of Islam, then unity and peacefulness will be destroyed. These evil qualities and actions will cause divisions and separations, and this Holy City will be taken from our hands, that is certain."

"When this happens, the followers of Islam will be as numerous as the granules of flour in dough. But the number of those who shall take possession of the city will be as few as the grains of salt in the dough. This will happen when degradation permeates Islam."

These were the words of 'Omar Ibn al-Khattab when he took possession of the Holy City and the sacred ground of the Dome of the Rock.

We must realize that if man wants peace and justice in the world and in his life, then he himself must conduct his life with good qualities. That is the only way man will find peace anywhere. All human society must realize this. Each one of us should reflect and understand what we must do. We must develop and strengthen our faith, certitude, and determination and look within.

Humor, wit and wisdom

The following are stories of a character named Nasserudin Mullah, who is said to have lived in Turkey. He may or may not be a fictional character, but either way the purpose here is to give a sampling of his wit and wisdom, something that has been passed on by generations. Hopefully it shows that Muslims too have a "lighter" side.

The Yogi, the Priest and the Sufi

Nasserudin Mulla put on a Sufi robe and decided to make a pious journey. On his way he met a priest and a yogi, and they decided to team up together. When they got to a village the others asked him to seek donations while they carried out their devotions. Nasserudin collected some money and bought halwa (a dessert) with it.

He suggested that they divide the food, but the others, who

112

were not yet hungry enough, said that it should be postponed until night. They continued on their way; and when night fell Nasserudin asked for the first portion 'because I was the means of getting the food'. The others disagreed: the priest on the grounds that he represented a properly organized hierarchical body, and should therefore have preference; the yogi because, he said, he ate only once in three days and should therefore have more.

Finally they decided to sleep. In the morning, the one who related the best dream should have first choice of halwa.

In the morning the priest said: 'In my dreams I saw the founder of my religion, who made a sign of benediction, singling me out as especially blessed.'

The others were impressed, but the yogi said: 'I dreamt that I visited Nirvana, and was utterly absorbed into nothing.'

They turned to the Mulla. 'I dreamt that I saw the Sufi teacher Khidr, who appears only to the most sanctified. 'He said: "Nasserudin, eat the halwa-now!" And, of course, I had to obey.'

Invisible extension

Nasserudin Mulla saw a man selling a beautifully made sword in the market. 'How can a piece of steel be worth fifty gold pieces?' he asked.

The auctioneer saw that he was no connoisseur of art and said: 'This is a magical sword. In battle it stretches itself by several feet and outreaches the enemy.' Within minutes the Mulla was back with a pair of fire tongs. 'Sell these,' he told the auctioneer, 'and note that the reserve price is a hundred gold pieces.'

'I hardly think that you will get more than a few coppers for these,' said the man.

'Nonsense said the Mulla. 'They may appear to be ordinary enough tongs. But when my wife throws them at me, even from thirty feet, they leap across the gap, invisibly extended.'

Rumi a Spiritual Journey from the Sufis

Sufis are Muslims who focus on being spiritually oriented using self-discipline. Sufism is not a sect, so there are both Sunni Sufis and Shia Sufis. The Sufi's goal is to combine their deep faith to reach a state of enlightenment by chanting and meditating on God and living lives of simplicity. Jalaluddin Rumi (1207 –1273) is perhaps one of the most popular Sufi poets, who has been rediscovered in the West. Others include Abdul Qadir Jailani, Rabi'a al Adwiya, Muhiyuddin ibn Arabi and Fakhruddin 'Iraqi. The following are some of Rumis most thought provoking couplets.

The Divine

For the lovers of God He alone is the source of all joy and sorrow, he alone is the true object of desire, every other kind of love is idol infatuation. Love for God is that flame which, when it blazes, burns away everything except God. Love for God is a sword, which cuts down all that is not of God. God alone is eternal; all else will vanish. (Masnavi V 586-590)

The Human Spirit

Your physical attributes, like your body are merely borrowed. Do not set your heart on them, for they are transient and only last for an hour. Your spirit by contrast is eternal; your body is on the earth, like a lamp, but its light comes from that everlasting source from above. (Masnavi IV 1840-1842)

The spiritual world

God's purpose for man is to acquire a seeing eye and an understanding heart. (Divan-I Shams 10906)

A Life Beyond

What do you really possess? And what have you gained in this life? What pearls have you brought from the depths of the sea? On the day of death, your physical senses will vanish. Do you have the spiritual light to illuminate your heart? What just fills your eyes in the grave, will your grave shine brightly? (Masnavi II 939-941)

A Life of Faith

When you put a cargo on aboard a ship, you make that venture on trust. For you do not know whether you will be drowned or safely reach the other shore. If you say, "I will not embark till I am certain of my fate," then you will do no trade: the secret of these two destinies is never disclosed. The faint-hearted merchant neither gains nor looses; nay he looses, for he is deprived of his fortune. Only those who are zealous in their search, who faithfully seek the flame, find the light. Since all affairs turn upon hope, surely faith is the worthiest object of hope, for thereby you win salvation. (Masnavi 3083-3091)

Free Will

Free will only leads to good by someone who has self-control and who fears God. (Masnavi V 642-655)

Muslim Converts: Their Stories

Convert or Revert, but by Choice

As every child that is born according to Muslim belief is born in a state of purity (called Fitrah) which naturally inclines to God, people who later in their lives decide to become Muslim say they are reverting to the Muslim faith. After all, a Muslim is one who submits to God. In other cases, e.g. African Americans, many of whose fore-fathers were also Muslim (e.g. Alex Haley, author of Roots who traces his lineage back to Kunta Kinte a Muslim) feel they are reverting to Islam. Islam is the fastest growing religion in America and in Western Europe, in countries like England, France, and Germany. Although people from all across the spectrum - men, women, white and black - become Muslims, what's interesting is that both in the United States and England the number of women who convert to Islam is far greater than men. Some ratios place it as high as four women to one man becoming Muslim. Most of these women are college educated, which again to the average American and in fact to most people would seem like an anomaly, considering how women and their rights are portrayed by the media.

It is important to know that Muslims do not recruit converts,

117

and there is no parallel to missionary work. Every Muslim is a Muslim by his or her own choice; so you will not find Muslims knocking on your door preaching religion.

Gary Miller

Whether you are thinking of converting, looking for information for a school project or are merely curious, welcome. Welcome to a world that may be familiar or unfamiliar, hated or loved, often misunderstood - depending on who you are and what you have been taught but when analyzed with pure intentions, it never fails to pleasantly surprise - regardless of who you are and what you've been taught. Islam is for every single human being that walks this earth - whether you are sick or healthy, rich or poor. If you are one who holds prejudices against this religion, someone who loves to hate and condemn, then, a renowned convert, Gary Miller has these words to say to you...

There is no compulsion for man to accept truth. But it is certainly a shame upon the human intellect when man is not even interested in finding out what the truth is. Islam teaches that God has given us the faculty of reason and therefore expects man to reason things out objectively and systematically for ourselves - to reflect and to question.

Nobody should press you to make a hasty decision to accept the teachings of Islam, for Islam teaches that humans should be given the freedom to choose. Even when a person is faced with the truth, there is no compulsion upon them to embrace it.

But before you begin to form an opinion about Islam, ask yourself, whether your existing knowledge of Islam is thorough enough. Ask yourself whether that knowledge has been obtained through non-Muslim third party sources who themselves have probably been exposed to only random glimpses of Islamic writings and have yet to reason on Islam objectively and systematically themselves.

1. A medical encyclopedia published in Chicago, Illinois, U.S.A., mentions Prophet Muhammad's name among those famous people who were epileptic.

2. A church publication in 1981 mentions the rise of Islam in

its early period in the following words: "…The moral looseness of the new faith, the might of the sword, the fanaticism of the new religion, the shrewdness of Muhammad, the hope of plunder, the love of wealth, the idea of a sensual paradise have been among the causes for the spread of Islam which today embraces one sixth of the world's population."

3. A fourth grade history text book published in U.S.A. has an article about Prophet Muhammad with the title, "a camel driver." The same article tells children 9 to 10 years of age about the status of women in Islam in the following words: "They believe that women should be slaves to men and that they thought a man might have as many wives as he wished, all at one time." The author tells children about the spread of Islam, "...very soon they began to force others to become Moslems whether they wanted or not. Like the highway robber who says, "Money or your life", they gave everyone a choice, "Money or your life, or be a Muslim."

Is it fair that one should form an opinion about the taste of a particular dish just by hearsay from others who may themselves not necessarily have tasted the dish yet? Similarly, you should find out for yourself about Islam from reliable opinion.

That would be an intellectual approach to Islam. It is up to you to make the next move - to realize the truth, reality and purpose of your existence. In making your move, Islam continuously reassures you that your rights to freedom of choice and freedom to use that God given faculty of thought and reason will be respected. Every man has that individual will. No one else can take away that will and force you to surrender to the will of God.

You will have to find and make that decision yourself.

Muslims in the United States

Islam is especially growing in the United States. However, it is difficult to generalize about American Muslims. They are indigenous and immigrants, factory workers and CEOs. This varied community is unified by a common faith, underpinned by a nationwide network of a large number of masjids (mosques). Muslims arrived early in North America, the first mosque being built in North Dakota in the 1920's. By the eighteenth century there were many native-born Muslims in North America. Great numbers of indigenous Americans have entered the fold of Islam. They are from different classes; the rich, the poor, the educated and the illiterate. Today, there are over six million Muslims in the United States; and some accounts have Islam as the second largest religion in the United States, surpassing even Judaism in its numbers.

It is well known that in the United States, Islam is the fastest-growing religion. The following are some observations on this phenomenon:

"Islam is the fastest-growing religion in America, a guide and pillar of stability for many of our people..." (Hillary Rodham Clinton, Los Angeles Times).

"Moslems are the world's fastest-growing group..." (The Population Reference Bureau, USA Today).

"...Islam is the fastest-growing religion in the country." (Geraldine Baum; Newsday Religion Writer, Newsday).

"Islam, the fastest-growing religion in the United States..." (Ari L.Goldman, New York Times).

Native American Muslims

The Message, July 1996

My name is Mahir Abdal-Razzaaq and I am a Cherokee Blackfoot American Indian who is Muslim. I am known as Eagle Sun Walker. I serve as a Pipe Carrier Warrior for the Northeastern Band of Cherokee Indians in New York City.

There are other Muslims in our group. For the most part, not many people are aware of the Native American contact with Islam that began over one thousand years ago by some of the early Muslim travelers who visited us. Some of these Muslim travelers ended up living among our people.

For most Muslims and non-Muslims of today, this type of information is unknown and has never been mentioned in any of the history books. There are many documents, treaties, legislation and resolutions that were passed between 1600s and 1800s that show that Muslims were in fact here and were very active in the communities in which they lived. Treaties such as Peace and Friendship that was signed on the Delaware River in the year 1787 bear the signatures of Abdel-Khak and Muhammad Ibn Abdullah. This treaty details our continued right to exist as a community in the areas of commerce, maritime shipping, current form of government at that time which was in accordance with Islam. According to a federal court case from the Continental Congress, we help put the breath of life in to the newly framed constitution. All of the documents are presently in the National Archives as well as the Library of Congress.

If you have access to records in the state of South Carolina, read the Moors Sundry Act of 1790. In a future article, God-willing, I will go into more details about the various tribes, their languages; in which some are influenced by Arabic, Persian, and Hebrew words. Almost all of the tribes vocabulary include the word Allah. The traditional dress code for Indian women includes the kimah and long dresses. For men, standard fare is turbans and long tops that come down to the knees. If you were to look at any of the old books on Cherokee clothing up until the time of 1832, you will see the men wearing turbans and the women wearing long head coverings. The last Cherokee chief who had a Muslim name was Ramadhan Ibn Wati of the Cherokees in 1866.

Cities across the United States and Canada bear names that are of Indian and Islamic derivation. Have you ever wondered what the name Tallahassee means? It means that He Allah will deliver you sometime in the future.

Malik

Becoming Muslim

The journey of a thousand miles has to start with the first step and this is the first part of my journey.

My name is Malik Muhammad Hassan and I have recently converted to Islam. When I was in junior high school I was first introduced to Islam by reading the book "Roots" by Alex Haley. It taught me a little bit about the strong will that most Muslims possess, myself included. It also introduced me to Allah. I had never heard of Allah in his real form until I read that book and I was very curious. I then started reading about "The Nation Of Islam" (specifically Malcolm X) and it fascinated me how devoted he was to Allah, especially after he left the self-serving Nation Of Islam. Reading about Malcolm made me think about a God who (for a change) did not have any physical form or limitations and, being a totally blind person, it made me relate to these people: the people who Malcolm and Haley referred to as Muslims. I continued reading what I could about Islam, which wasn't as much as it should have been. My reading material was very limited because like I said above: I am a totally blind person and the material available about Islam in Braille or on tape was not only very little, but also very general. I believe the reason was that the material that I had access to wasn't written by Muslims and it kind of painted a dark picture of Islam. I think most of the literature written by Christians or non-Muslims about Islam tends to do that most of the time. And I didn't know that there were even Muslims in Halifax so I obviously didn't know any. I didn't even know about the local Islamic association until I was already a Muslim.

So, I read what I could until my first year out of high school around the month of May, 1996, when I received a phone call asking me if I wanted to participate in a camp for blind and visually impaired people known throughout Canada as Score. I agreed and sent them a resume and praise be to Allah I was accepted for work.

At first I really didn't want to go but something kept telling me it would be a good idea if I went. So, on June 30th 1996 I boarded a plane from Nova Scotia to Toronto and took my last trip as a non-Muslim; I just didn't know it yet.

I got to Toronto and everything at first was pretty normal... It was on the second day that I was there when the journey of a thousand miles first started.

I arrived on a Sunday and on the next day I met the person who Allah would use with His divine power to help guide me to the beautiful Religion of Islam. I met a sister named Rizvana and if she reads this I hope she doesn't get mad at me for using her name.

When I met her, I immediately wanted to talk to her because I liked her name. I asked her of what origin her name was and she told me that it was Arabic; so I asked her if she was Muslim and she replied with the answer of yes. I immediately started telling her what I already knew about Islam which lasted about ten seconds. I started asking her questions and also asking her to talk to me about Islam.

One particular incident that comes to my mind is when all of the workers at the camp went to a baseball game and the sister and I started talking about Islam and missed pretty much the whole game.

Well, anyways, we talked for about three, maybe four days on and off about Islam and on July the fifth if my memory doesn't fail me I became a Muslim. My life has been totally different ever since. I look at things very differently than I used to and I finally feel like I belong to a family. All Muslims are brothers and sisters in Islam so I could say that I have approximately 1.2 billion brothers and sisters all to whom I'm proud to be related. I finally know what it feels like to be humble and to worship a God that I don't have to see.

For any non-Muslim reading this just look at it this way. It's good to learn, but you never know when you will be tested and if you're not in the class at the time of the final exam no matter how much you know you'll never get any credit. If you want to get credit sign up for the class. In other words, declare shahada (testimony to faith) and let Allah teach you everything you need to know. Believe me the reward is worth it. You could say the reward is literally heaven.

If any good comes out of this story all the credit is due to Allah; only the mistakes are my own.

I would like to mention a part of a hadith that has had a great effect on me and that is:

"Worship Allah as if you see him and if you don't see him, know that he sees you." – Sahih Muslim, Volume 1, Number 1

Ruqqaya

I learned of Islam while in high school back in the 1970's... I was raised as a Christian in the Baptist faith, went to church religiously, even studied the catholic creed.. thought I wanted to be a nun. I just could not find the rationale and peace in Christianity.. many questions were never answered.. just told to be afraid of hell.. Christ would redeem us.. always questioned.. why was Jesus crucified and no one else? why was Jesus / god white? how can three be one and the same? questioned the trinity? I was first attracted to a Muslim sister I saw on the train at 16 years old. She had an aura that was beautiful. I made a promise to myself that one day I wanted to be like her. Only Allah knew what would have become of me..He was merciful.. I am Muslim now 22 years. al hamdu lilah (All Praise is to God).

Colonel Donald S. Rockwell

(Poet, Critic & Author)

The simplicity of Islam, the powerful appeal and the compelling atmosphere of its mosques, the earnestness of its faithful adherents, the confidence inspiring realization of the millions throughout the world who answer the five daily calls to prayer- these factors attracted me from the first. But after I had determined to become a follower of Islam, I found many deeper reasons for confirming my decision.

The mellow concept of life — fruit of the Prophet's combined course of action and contemplation —- the wise counsel, the admonitions to charity and mercy, the broad humanitarianism, the pioneer declaration of woman's property rights - these and other factors of the teachings of the man of Mecca were to me among the most obvious evidence of a practical religion so tersely and so aptly epitomized in the cryptic words of Muhammad, "Trust in God and tie your camel". He gave us a religious system of normal action, not blind faith in the protection of an unseen force in spite of our own neglect, but confidence that if we do all things rightly and to the best of our ability, we may trust in what comes as the Will of God.

The broadminded tolerance of Islam for other religions recommends it to all lovers of liberty. Muhammad admonished his followers to treat well the believers in the Old and New Testaments; and Abraham, Moses and Jesus are acknowledged as co-prophets of the One God. Surely this is generous and far in advance of the attitude of other religions.

The total freedom from idolatry ... is a sign of the salubrious strength and purity of the Muslim faith. The original teachings of the Prophet of God have not been engulfed in the maze of changes and additions of doctrinarians. The Quran remains as it came to the corrupt polytheistic people of Muhammad's time, changeless as the holy heart of Islam itself.

Moderation and temperance in all things, the keynotes of Islam, won my unqualified approbation. The health of his people was cherished by the Prophet, who enjoined them to observe strict cleanliness and specified fasts and to subordinate carnal appetites ... when I stood in the inspiring mosques of Istanbul, Damascus, Jerusalem, Cairo, Algiers, Tangier, Fez and other cities, I was conscious of a powerful reaction [to] the potent uplift of Islam's simple appeal to the sense of higher things, unaided by elaborate trappings, ornamentations, figures, pictures, music and ceremonial ritual. The mosque is a place of quiet contemplation and self-effacement in the greater reality of the One God.

The democracy of Islam has always appealed to me. Potentate and pauper have the same rights on the floor of the mosque, on their knees in humble worship. There are no rented pews nor special reserved seats.

The Muslim accepts no man as a mediator between himself and his God. He goes direct to the invisible source of creation and life, God, without reliance on saving formula of repentance of sins and belief in the power of a teacher to afford him salvation.

The universal brotherhood of Islam, regardless of race, politics, color or country, has been brought home to me most keenly many times in my life and this is another feature which drew me towards the Faith.

America Land of Plenty, Land of Poverty: What Islam has to offer the World

Today the United States is the greatest military, political, technological, economic, and media power in the world. Yet all this material greatness and excellence has robbed it, us, and all the societies that we influence, of the mores and values that are the bedrock of any society. In the last half of the twentieth century, we are being plagued by social unrest, from alcoholism to drug addiction, sexual permissiveness in general, to adultery, teen pregnancies and AIDS; pornography and prostitution to violent crimes including pedophilia, rape, sexual harassment and homicides, poverty, divorce, and suicide. The list is endless. Material society has made us slaves to our lowest desires.

Erich Fromm in "On Being Human" says that the disease from which modern man suffers is alienation, which is caused by "idolatry." The idolater is a person who prays to the products of his own hands... and modern man is constituted by the things he creates. We believe that we control, yet we are being controlled-not by a tyrant, but by things, by circumstances. We have become humans without will or aim. We talk of progress and of the future, although in reality no one knows where he is going, and no one says where things are going to, and no one has a goal. One of the major challenges of materialism is the mantra, leave unto God what is God's and unto Caesar what is Caesar's, leave the economy to the economists, banking to the bankers, law creation to the politicians. However, the world is an interconnected world, all aspects of life, whether they be personal, family, work or social are interconnected, as is the human body. Without having faith (Iman) and being God Conscious (having Taqwa) any solution to a problem with even the best of intentions will fall short. This is why for example Prohibition (of Alcohol) in the United States failed, whereas the Prohibition sent in the Quranic revelation and practiced by the Prophet Muhammad and his followers succeeded. The root of one evil when eliminated prevents so many others. In our age this means no alcohol related deaths, family breakups due to alcoholism, health problems, addiction in general and more.

The only way to free ourselves is to go back to the Creator's guidance. The power of Islam is to transform human beings, to change society, to alter the way we perceive reality, and to take that perception out to those who are still enchained in the delusion of this world. This is Islam. As Islam is based on tawhid (oneness of God), no problem can be seen in isolation. Problems-solutions, cause-effect are not only simplistic viewpoints they are not from the Quranic vocabulary. The Quran talks about those who have diseases in their hearts and that the Quran is the healing for that which is in their breasts.

Islam has, when viewed from today's Western standards, a strong and what may appear to be an extreme view of moral conduct by some. For example, in terms of sexual morality, adultery is seen (as in the previous scriptures) as a great sin, the punishment of which is death. Islam prohibits men and women to mix freely and casually (intermingling). Not only is adultery a sin, but also any path that can lead to it has to be avoided.

"And come not close to adultery. Verily it is a great sin and evil way." (17:32)

Through the media you may get the impression that suicide, especially "suicide bombings," is looked upon highly. In reality suicide is absolutely prohibited. All good things that a human possesses, including their body, spouse, children and wealth are a trust. So it is a major sin to break this trust as life is given and taken only by God. The Prophet Muhammad has said to the effect that however a person kills himself, that act will keep on repeating itself and the person will be thrown in hell fire.

Each time a violent crime, especially on a large scale, e.g. murder-suicide or mass shootings in schools and workplaces takes place we become angry at the gun manufacturers, or those who make violent films, or video games. After the commotion has died and some lip-service paid the pattern repeats itself. When criminals are caught and sentenced their likelihood of being repeat criminals is very high. Once again it is society that pays the price. Each additional murder, rape or abuse that takes place is one too many. One of the interesting facts is that a significant number of inmates become Muslim while in prison. The vast majority are transformed and reformed, with repeat offenses once they are out-side being much lower. The underlying theme being that Islam has the power to transform humanity to a better state.

Islam shows the believer to be God-conscious, socially con-scious, and morally conscious.

The Quran says "The most honorable among you in the sight of God is the one who is the most God Conscious." (49:13). Social consciousness is based on specific acts of kindness to par-ents, spouses, relatives, neighbors, and those who fall under a per-son's jurisdiction. Morality is expressed in the Quran in terms of equality, justice, fairness, brotherhood, mercy, compassion, soli-darity, and freedom of choice. Individual responsibility is a cor-nerstone of Islam as every Muslim (and human being) is account-able for what they do and fail to do. Those in leadership roles have a greater accountability, which goes beyond the individual accountability to God and the people.

Life from an Islamic perspective is very serious, as it is based on our individual actions and intentions that we will be judged. Life is a blessing so no one should think life is not worth living. Life has a purpose. We have not been created in vain, and so no one should be letting it go by aimlessly. The human being has both a physical and spiritual component. Until and unless human life is regulated by the belief in God and obedience to His laws, the human will be at best materially rich and spiritually poor. Now that we have conquered outer space we need to address the inner space. With the business world being rocked by major companies who have committed "creative accounting" practices, ending up in fraud and bankruptcy, not only are financial audits required but so are social and moral audits. If greed, avarice, and the "market" become the idols that we worship then the greater danger is a lack of trust in the system and society which can lead to not only finan-cial bankruptcy but also spiritual and moral bankruptcy.

Family and legitimate children are the foundations of society. The break up of families through divorce has reached epidemic proportions. It is a well- known fact that more than half of first time marriages in the West end up in divorce. The instability that this brings to both husband, wife and even more to children cannot be measured. Although divorce is permitted in Islam, the Prophet Muhammad said that "of all the permitted things, divorce is the most hated to God." Although the causes of divorce can be many, the focus here is that anything that can lead to family instability, eg extra-marital affairs, needs to be addressed head on and those areas where family communications breakdown need to be addressed through reconciliation.

In reality, Islam avoids the extremes of celibacy and sexual promiscuity. It has a healthy view of sex, which if seen in the bigger context can help avoid the social diseases and crimes that are becoming rampant. The Prophet Muhammad prohibited a man or a woman (who are not related either by marriage or a family relationship eg brother-sister) to be in the same room, as their companion is Satan (who can mislead them). Similarly no adult should be alone with an unrelated child. Women and men when they do interact must do so in modesty, both are asked to lower the gaze and to dress modestly to avoid physical attraction, which may lead to sexual desire.

"Tell the believing men to lower their gaze and guard their sexuality: that is purer for them indeed. God is aware of what they do. And tell the believing women to lower their gaze and guard their sexuality." (24:30-31)

"O Prophet, tell your wives and your daughters and the believing women that they should draw their outer garments over themselves (while going out of their houses), this will help them to be distinguished (from other women who make a display of their beauty and ornamentation) so as not to be annoyed. And Allah is Oft forgiving and Most Merciful." (33:59).

Most parts of the Muslim world have separate sections for women to accommodate them in schools, hospitals, transportation and other public facilities where men may come into contact with women. Male guests are entertained by the male host and in a separate part of the home women gather. The dress of a Muslim woman reflects modesty. This for those who reflect back on history should not be a surprise, as traditional women in this culture and others, including Nuns dressed modestly, covering most of their body. Any necessary contact between unrelated men and women has to be at an intellectual level as opposed to a physical level. A woman is not public property, to be used as a sum total of body parts to promote the wares of man, from consumer goods to any thing that sells. Islam came to liberate humanity and especially those in society who were weak and exploited, especially women. Every woman, and for that matter human being has the right to self-dignity and self-respect which no one should be allowed to exploit.

All intoxicants including alcohol and gambling are forbidden in Islam. "9's plan is (but) to excite enmity and hatred among you, with intoxicants and gambling, and to turn you away from the remembrance of Allah and from prayer: Will you not then abstain (5:90-91)

The character and role model for the Muslim is the Prophet Muhammad. In a narration, he said the following which describes His character, and that the Muslim tries to emulate. This narration gives a complete picture of the human being that Islam hopes to build.

"Nine things the Lord has commanded me:

1. Fear of God in private and in public;
2. Justness, whether in anger or in calmness;
3. Moderation in both poverty and affluence;
4. Joining hands with those who break away from me;
5. And giving to those who deprive me;
6. And forgiving those who wrong me;
7. And making my silence mediation;
8. And my words remembrance of God;
9. And taking a lesson from my observation.

To summarize,

Although we in the US and in the West in general live in a material land of plenty, it is the spiritual poverty that has robbed us of our collective morality. While we scare ourselves to death of international terrorism, we are being succumbed by domestic terrorism, the only problem is that we do not see each of these heinous social crimes as terrorism. Every lost child, every women who is robbed of her dignity, every man who has his life taken unnecessarily is a victim to these acts of mini-terrorism. The net result of these is far more destructive than anything that we have seen from Pearl Harbor to the September 11th attacks. The collateral damage is seen in the daily local news.

Life, liberty, the pursuit of happiness, one nation under God, these are some of our most cherished values. If we are to retain them, please take another look at what Islam has to offer the world. Like-minded people need to come together, to join hands, to address a common problem, which has a common solution. For society to move in a positive direction the challenges mentioned need to be addressed. They may seem daunting, but without addressing them they will not only destroy our inner cities, but also suburbia, and the heartlands of America and the world. Materialism knows no boundaries. People in leadership roles, whether they be in business, politics, or at any level need to be the sources of light that others will look up to. The goal here is not to make America or Western Europe a theocracy, just to allow us to return to the values that we've been founded on. Let us come together, to start a culture of dialog which can help rebuild the spirit of justice and inner uprightness.

CONCLUSION ISLAM 101:

Islam 101 has been an attempt to introduce Islam for contemporary times, to explain the beliefs and practices of Islam and to address two of the most common myths regarding the status of women and jihad. The purpose has been to allow in a very rudimentary way a means to dialogue, to pave the way to understanding. In Islam, faith and reason do come together, science and religion come together, so observing nature and reflecting on God's presence and power come together. Can the heavens and earth work in perfect harmony without the one Creator, the one God? Muslims believe that all people will answer to this same one God, regardless of race or religion. The Prophet Muhammad narrated "People are equal, like the teeth of a comb. You are all from Adam; and Adam is from dust. There is no superiority of white over black, nor of Arab over non-Arab, except by piety." Therein lies the essence of how humans will be judged, by actions. Again another prophetic narrative, "Allah does not look at your bodies and figures, but looks at your hearts and deeds."

Although there are many ways by which we can differentiate ourselves, the focus of Islam101 is first to build common ground. Islam shares a common origin with Judaism and Christianity. A common belief in the One and same God, in Abraham as the father of prophets. Islam-by-in-large in the West is presented as something very alien, yet no connection is made that the God of Adam, Abraham, Moses, and Jesus is the same God of Muhammad, may peace be upon them all. Their fundamental message was the same - to worship one God. In fact Islam is an Arabic word which means submission to God and is derived from the word peace, a central element of Islam. There is only one source of peace. When one submits, they are at peace with God, at peace with oneself, and at peace with God's creation.

Although this book has tried to address two of the most common myths regarding jihad and the status of women, the reality is that there will continue to be an avalanche of news regarding Islamic fundamentalism, terrorism, and oppressed women.

If one believes in the fundamentals of faith, then in a way they are a fundamentalist. The fundamentals of Islam start with its source it's teachings, which are the Quran, which was revealed to prophet Muhammad and his teachings, the Hadith. The fundamentals of Islamic practice rest on five pillars starting with declaring the Oneness of God and the finality of the prophet-hood of Muhammad, praying five times a day, fasting in the month of Ramadan, in giving charity to the needy and making the once-in-a-lifetime journey of pilgrimage to Mecca. It is fundamental in Islam to believe in all the prophets including Moses and Jesus, and the books revealed to them, the angels, the day of judgment (including the after life) and supremacy of God's will.

The "evil empire" of the Soviet Union and Communism has been replaced by the "axis of evil", which points all fingers (and toes) to Islam. It is important to remember that jihad means struggle in God's path. Struggle against many forms including internal temptations and external oppression. When conditions necessitate war, it can be only be sanctioned by a qualified leader, its purpose is to strive for peace and justice, to defend oneself or to remove human tyranny. This struggle can only be on the battlefield and not against civilians or the environment. In terms of the status of women, the text has covered that Islam came to liberate woman from oppression and has given her rights which are unparalleled in their completeness of fairness and equality. The relationship of husband and wife is based on love and compassion. The Prophet Muhammad in a narration said "The best of you are those who are most kind to their wives, and I am the best amongst you." The interaction between men and women is based on modesty. The dress, eye contact and other behavior means men and women deal with each other on a spiritual as opposed to a physical level, which frees the practicing Muslim from the social and criminal crimes which are becoming so rampant in society.

It is important to make the distinction that Islam is the religion and Muslims are those who believe in and practice the religion. As in every society there are those who understand and practice the faith according to the letter and spirit of the law and then those who fall astray. It is unfair to take a faith of over a billion people and based on the actions of a few, characterize and condemn one fifth of the world's population.

Muslims are of every race and nationality and an integral part of many societies as a majority or as minorities. No matter how diverse the Muslims are, they have the same hopes and dreams as the rest of humanity. Muslims are proud of the rich cultural heritage and the contributions they have made to civilization. As people who are proud of their beliefs and principles, Muslims are not out to conquer the world, or to force their beliefs on anyone and everyone. There are, however, legacy issues especially from the post-colonial world, where inequities need to be addressed. Equity is to justice what justice is to peace and each is intricately linked. The Islamic way of life has much to offer both Muslims and the rest of the world. Ultimately, Muslims have to demonstrate what Islam really means in the era we live in, and those of other faiths and cultures need to allow for a culture of dialogue, a culture of empathy, and a culture of forgiveness.

So now that Islam 101 has concluded where do we go from here? If we are to develop this culture of dialog and understanding, then we must make use of all paths that are available. At a personal level this could mean meeting and getting to know practicing Muslims in whichever environment you are in, from businesses to colleges, from neighbors to co-workers, and by visiting local mosques. There are organizations you can get involved with, or invite, including CAMP (Christians and Muslims for Peace) working on bridge-building and ING (Islamic Networks Group) which have speakers bureaus to address middle and high school students in the US. You can further you own knowledge of Islam by reading some of the books and visiting the websites mentioned in the reference section. You can supplement your news, by getting more independent news from alternative media, and even when getting news from the mainstream media just by being more objective and critical. See how the news and media coverage, placement and positioning differ about Islam and Muslims when compared with other events and faiths? It is valid to ask, when a news story breaks out, what is the significance of this over other events, who stands to benefit from this, and if things don't make sense to reply to the editor of the source.

Islam 101 in part has been about building bridges of under-standing. So I will leave you with what I hope is a thought-pro-voking story. The Arabs tell a story about a Grammarian and a Ferryman. The Grammarian was making a crossing on the ferry, and asked the ferryman if he knew grammar. The ferryman replied in the negative, so the grammarian said "You have wasted half of your life." Later in the crossing a storm approached, the boat began to take in water and sink. The ferryman asked the grammarian if he knew how to swim. The grammarian replied in the negative, so the ferryman replied "You have wasted all of your life." Perceptions determine our realities, let's make them based on mutual understanding.

Salam (Peace)

APENDIX A

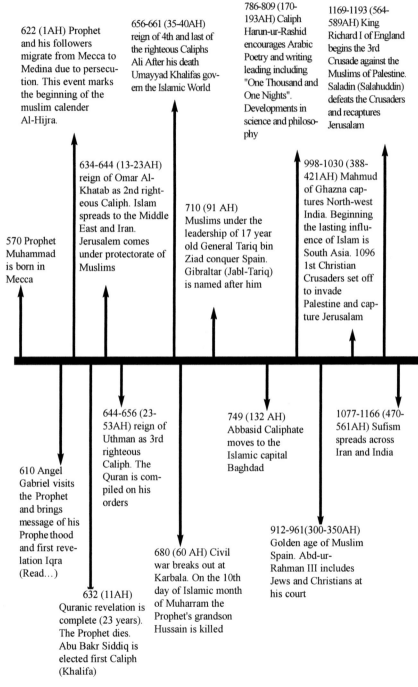

622 (1AH) Prophet and his followers migrate from Mecca to Medina due to persecution. This event marks the beginning of the muslim calender Al-Hijra.

656-661 (35-40AH) reign of 4th and last of the righteous Caliphs Ali After his death Umayyad Khalifas govern the Islamic World

786-809 (170-193AH) Caliph Harun-ur-Rashid encourages Arabic Poetry and writing leading including "One Thousand and One Nights". Developments in science and philosophy

1169-1193 (564-589AH) King Richard I of England begins the 3rd Crusade against the Muslims of Palestine. Saladin (Salahuddin) defeats the Crusaders and recaptures Jerusalam

634-644 (13-23AH) reign of Omar Al-Khatab as 2nd righteous Caliph. Islam spreads to the Middle East and Iran. Jerusalem comes under protectorate of Muslims

710 (91 AH) Muslims under the leadership of 17 year old General Tariq bin Ziad conquer Spain. Gibraltar (Jabl-Tariq) is named after him

998-1030 (388-421AH) Mahmud of Ghazna captures North-west India. Beginning the lasting influence of Islam is South Asia. 1096 1st Christian Crusaders set off to invade Palestine and capture Jerusalam

570 Prophet Muhammad is born in Mecca

610 Angel Gabriel visits the Prophet and brings message of his Prophethood and first revelation Iqra (Read...)

644-656 (23-53AH) reign of Uthman as 3rd righteous Caliph. The Quran is compiled on his orders

749 (132 AH) Abbasid Caliphate moves to the Islamic capital Baghdad

1077-1166 (470-561AH) Sufism spreads across Iran and India

632 (11AH) Quranic revelation is complete (23 years). The Prophet dies. Abu Bakr Siddiq is elected first Caliph (Khalifa)

680 (60 AH) Civil war breaks out at Karbala. On the 10th day of Islamic month of Muharram the Prophet's grandson Hussain is killed

912-961(300-350AH) Golden age of Muslim Spain. Abd-ur-Rahman III includes Jews and Christians at his court

Timeline of Important Event in Islamic History

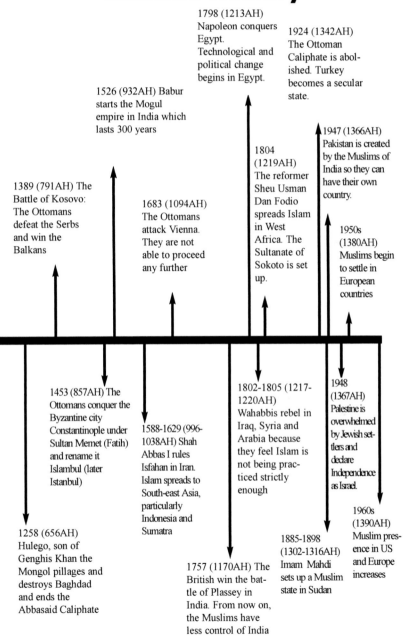

1798 (1213AH) Napoleon conquers Egypt. Technological and political change begins in Egypt.

1924 (1342AH) The Ottoman Caliphate is abolished. Turkey becomes a secular state.

1526 (932AH) Babur starts the Mogul empire in India which lasts 300 years

1947 (1366AH) Pakistan is created by the Muslims of India so they can have their own country.

1389 (791AH) The Battle of Kosovo: The Ottomans defeat the Serbs and win the Balkans

1683 (1094AH) The Ottomans attack Vienna. They are not able to proceed any further

1804 (1219AH) The reformer Sheu Usman Dan Fodio spreads Islam in West Africa. The Sultanate of Sokoto is set up.

1950s (1380AH) Muslims begin to settle in European countries

1453 (857AH) The Ottomans conquer the Byzantine city Constantinople under Sultan Memet (Fatih) and rename it Islambul (later Istanbul)

1588-1629 (996-1038AH) Shah Abbas I rules Isfahan in Iran. Islam spreads to South-east Asia, particularly Indonesia and Sumatra

1802-1805 (1217-1220AH) Wahabbis rebel in Iraq, Syria and Arabia because they feel Islam is not being practiced strictly enough

1948 (1367AH) Palestine is overwhelmed by Jewish settlers and declare Independence as Israel.

1960s (1390AH) Muslim presence in US and Europe increases

1258 (656AH) Hulego, son of Genghis Khan the Mongol pillages and destroys Baghdad and ends the Abbasaid Caliphate

1757 (1170AH) The British win the battle of Plassey in India. From now on, the Muslims have less control of India

1885-1898 (1302-1316AH) Imam Mahdi sets up a Muslim state in Sudan

APENDIX B
Muslim world Population

Country / entity	Capital	Population (Millions)
Afghanistan	Kabul	26.8
Albania	Tirana	3.5
Algeria	Algiers	31.7
Azerbaijan	Baku	7.8
Bahrain	Manama	0.6
Bangladesh	Dhaka	131.3
Bosnia and Herzegovina	Sarajevo	3.9
Brunei	Bandar Seri Begawan	0.3
Cameroon	Yaounde	15.8
Chad	N'Djamena	8.7
Djibouti	Djibouti	0.5
Egypt	Cairo	69.5
Gabon	Libreville	1.2
"Gambia, The"	Banjul	1.4
Gaza Strip	–	1.2
Ghana	Accra	19.9
Indonesia	Jakarta	228.4
Iran	Tehran	66.1
Iraq	Baghdad	23.3
Jordan	Amman	5.2
Kazakhstan	Astana	16.7
Kuwait	Kuwait	2.0
Kyrgyzstan	Bishkek	4.8
Lebanon	Beirut	3.6
Libya	Tripoli	5.2
Malaysia	Kuala Lumpur	22.2
Maldives	Male	0.3
Mali	Bamako	11.0
Mauritania	Nouakchott	2.7
Morocco	Rabat	30.6
Mozambique	Maputo	19.4
Niger	Niamey	10.4

Country / entity	Capital	Population (Millions)
Nigeria	Abuja	126.6
Oman	Muscat	2.6
Pakistan	Islamabad	144.6
Qatar	Doha	0.8
Saudi Arabia	Riyadh	22.8
Senegal	Dakar	10.3
Sierra Leone	Freetown	5.4
Somalia	Mogadishu	7.5
Sudan	Khartoum	36.1
Suriname	Paramaribo	0.4
Syria	Damascus	16.7
Tajikistan	Dushanbe	6.6
Togo	Lome	5.2
Tunisia	Tunis	9.7
Turkey	Ankara	66.5
Turkmenistan	Ashgabat	4.6
Uganda	Kampala	24.0
United Arab Emirates	Abu Dhabi	2.4
Uzbekistan	Tashkent	25.2
West Bank	–	2.1
Western Sahara	–	0.3
Yemen	Sanaa	18.1

Muslim	Population (M)	Total Population (M)	% Muslim
South Africa	0.9	43.5	2
Germany	1.4	83.0	1.7
UK	1.5	59.6	2.5
France	1.8	59.5	3
US	6	278.0	2.2
Russia	27.6	145.5	19
China	38.2	"1,273.3"	3
India	123.6	"1,029.9"	12

APPENDIX C : The Islamic Calendar

The Islamic calendar (Hijri) is based on the year the Prophet Muhammad and his companions emigrated from Mecca to the city of Medina to escape persecution in the year 622 C.E. This migration is called the Hijrah. The Islamic calendar is lunar, where each month begins with the sighting of the new moon. It shifts by approximately eleven days each year with respect to the Western Gregorian Calendar.

The Islamic Months

Muharram
Safar
Rabiul-Awwal
Rabi-uthani
Jumadi-ul-Awwal
Jumadi-uthani
Rajab
Sha'ban
Ramadan (month of fasting)
Shawwal
Dhil-Q'ada
Dhil-Hijja (month of Pilgrimage)

Major celebrations and days of importance are:

9 &10th Muharram: Ashura: Day of fasting and forgiveness
12th Rabiul-Awwal: Birth date of the Prophet
27th Rajab: Laylat al-Miraj: Night journey of the Prophet
21st, 23rd, 25th, 27th, 29th Ramadan: Night of Power
1st Shawwal: Eid-ul Fitr (Festival at end of Ramadan)
9th Dhil-Hija: Arafat: day of standing and central of five days of pilgrimage
10th Dhil-Hija: Eid-ul Adha (Festival of Sacrifice after Hajj)

APPENDIX D : Guidelines for Employers, Schools, Neighbors & Media

The following are some general guidelines when interacting with Muslims. Guidelines are generalizations that help to develop an understanding of an area which is not known. In practice you will deal with individuals, so there is no one set of rules. Where possible it's always good to clarify and confirm what works for both of you. The more personally you can get to know Muslims, the better you can meet their needs and build a lasting relationship.

Guidelines regarding accommodating Muslim practices

Prayer has been covered under the five pillars section. In terms of understanding and accommodating a Muslim's prayer please be aware of the following:

There are five daily prayers at: dawn, mid-day, late-afternoon, sunset and nightfall.

Cleanliness of body and prayer location is very important in Islam. Before the prayer a ritual washing called wudu is done which means washing the face, arms and feet with clean water, usually in a bathroom sink. You can choose to observe, ignore, or comment "Looks like you're getting ready for prayer." Now that'll impress them!

In a mosque a call to prayer called the adhan is made. If you have seen any film or program on TV which depicts a Muslim land, you have probably heard this calling. As Muslims, especially men, are encouraged to pray together preferably in a mosque, the muazzin (person who calls the adhan) recites in a melodious voice the call to prayer in Arabic. This would be analogous to church bells calling the people to prayer.

Prayers must be performed in a clean dry place, free from distractions and facing Mecca, which is generally north east in the US. A prayer rug may be used, but this is not mandatory.

Each prayer is composed of distinct standing, bowing, prostrating, and sitting positions during which various prayers are read, including verses from the Quran. If you come across some one or a group in any of these positions, please do not interrupt them. Other than the prescribed prayer, no talking or distractions are allowed, so do not take offense or feel that the person is being rude.

Besides the five daily prayers, the noon prayer on Fridays called Jumah is offered as a congregational prayer. Muslims of a whole neighborhood or city depending on the size will gather together. This prayer is longer as it typically takes one hour due to the sermon, plus time taken to go to the mosque. In the workplace it's best to avoid early afternoon meetings as this can become a conflict. Due to daylight savings time the time does shift between winter and summer. Either way this translates to an extended lunch break.

Fasting also has been covered under the Five Pillars of Islam. As the Islamic calendar is based on the lunar month, both the start and end of Ramadan are marked by the new crescent moon. The lunar year shifts by 11 to 12 days each year compared to the Western calendar, so Ramadan eventually rotates through all the seasons. Muslims still continue with their daily activities of school, work, etc. When Ramadan is in winter the days and fasts are shorter, so Muslims usually have a preference to open their fast at home with their families and will skip lunch and may request their work hours to be shifted. Any accommodations are usually much appreciated. As a preference, fasting Muslims will usually prefer not to travel. Once again it's best to check with them.

Muslims who wish to perform the pilgrimage, Hajj which is obligatory once in a lifetime will usually request vacation time in advance. The Hajj is offered in the twelfth month of the Islamic calendar. A typical Hajj usually takes two to three weeks, due to both time taken in travel to Saudi Arabia as well as Muslims wanting to make the best of this the most sacred journey they will ever take.

The two major Muslim holidays are the two Eid's which mark the end of the month of Ramadan and the Hajj/Sacrifice. Muslims will usually take a day's vacation for each Eid if it falls during a workday.

To learn and teach more about Islam invite an employee who practices Islam to speak at a gathering for all employees or co-sponsor with other employers a community wide event to show the contributions of Islam. In other settings inviting a local imam or scholar of Islam may be more appropriate.

Islamic Protocol

Diet/catering/lunch guidelines when dealing with Muslims

1. Muslims eat only permitted (Halal) foods. Halal meat, also called Zabiha is very similar to the Jewish Kosher in the way the meat is "prepared". Muslims normally buy their meat from Muslim butchers. A general guideline is that pork and any by-product is forbidden. Lamb, chicken, and beef if Halal are OK. If going out to eat in a restaurant (if it is not offering Halal meats), the safest is seafood and vegetarian. The above is the general rule, the exception is that there are some Muslims who eat regular meat.

2. Halal food is not just defined by the kind of meat but also by the ingredients in the food. Some of the ingredients to watch out for are shortening, stock, lard, and any animal by-product.

3. Alcohol is forbidden in Islam. This includes not only beer, wines but also cooking wine, sherry and wine vinegar. It is not only a case of not drinking alcohol but most practicing Muslims will feel uncomfortable in any environment where alcohol is served.

4. Hygiene is very important in Islam. This includes for example the pre-washing before prayers, washing hands before eating meals, and before preparing food, including the cleanliness of the utensils that are used.

Dress

The general guideline for Muslims is to dress modestly. This applies to both men and women. The dress of women is more visible as it includes the hijab, which includes the head scarf and a loose coat and in a much smaller minority the face-veil. Hijab is a commandment in Islam given in the Quran and teachings of the Prophet Muhammad. Some Muslim women choose not to wear hijab for various reasons. Some may want to wear it but believe they cannot get a job wearing a head scarf. Others may not be aware of the requirement or are under the mistaken impression that wearing hijab is an indication of inferior status.

Men often times wear a skull cap (called kufi), or sometimes a turban. Devout Muslims also wear beards which are required to be clean and properly trimmed.

If you are invited to a Muslim house the general rule is to dress modestly.

Gender interaction and Social Events

Once again I must re-emphasize that every situation is unique. The general guideline is that men and women do not inter-mix and socialize as they do in other cultures. Where there is interaction, men and women are expected to lower their gaze, so maintaining eye contact is not a part of traditional culture and is discouraged in Islam. Similarly when men and women need to interact or meet they do not shake hands or come into physical contact. Many Muslims may be reluctant to participate in religious holidays of other faiths, social gatherings where there's intermingling, or where there is dancing, music and alcohol is served.

Guidelines for Schools:

(based on Islamic Society of North America Guidelines)

Muslim students in your school system should not be required to:

* Participate in plays, proms, social parties, picnics, dating, etc. which require free mixing of the two sexes.

* Participate in any event or activity related to Christmas, Easter, Halloween, or Valentine's Day. All such occasions have religious and social connotations contrary to Islamic faith and teachings.

* Sit next to the opposite sex in the classroom (if possible)

* Participate in physical education, swimming or dancing classes with the opposite sex.. Alternative meaningful education activities should be arranged for them. Please organize physical education and swimming classes separately for boys and girls in accordance with the following guidelines:

* Separate classes should be held for boys and girls in a fully covered area.

* Only female instructors for the respective group.

* Special swimming suits which will cover all the private parts of the body down to the knee.

* Separate and covered shower facilities for each student.

* They are excused from their classes to attend off-campus special prayers on Fridays (approximately 12:00 to 2:00 P.M.).

* They are excused for 15 minutes in the afternoon to offer a special prayer in a designated area on the Campus. This prayer is mandatory for all Muslims and often cannot be offered after the school hours.

* All food items containing meat of a pig in any form and shape as well as alcohol should be clearly labeled in the cafeteria.

* At least one properly covered toilet should be available in each men's and women's room.

* Muslim students are excused, without penalty of absence, for the two most important festivals of Islam: Eid al-Fitr and Eid al-Adha, in accordance with the lunar calendar.

To obtain information about texts and other useful resources including a Speakers bureau which make presentations to Middle and High school students contact the Council on Islamic Education or Islamic Networks Group (see Appendix for details).

Guidelines for the media on reporting about Islam or Muslims

(Courtesy of Islamic Networks Group)

* Apply one standard in reporting about religions. Focus on the particular person or group being discussed, rather than indicting all Muslims by the use of such terms as "Islamic terrorists" or "Islamic extremists". The media has never focused on the religious affiliations as such non-Muslim terrorists as Timothy McVeigh, the Columbine killers, or the Unabomber. Also, extremist anti-abortionists are not referred to as Christian terrorists, IRA members as Catholic terrorists, or Baruch Goldstein & other extremist Jewish settlers as Jewish terrorists.

* Report facts, not unsubstantiated theories. For example, when reporting about any Muslim suspect in the world, there is a growing tendency to automatically link them to Osama bin Laden, or any other group, known or unknown that "may" have terrorist connections. Insinuations and conjectures have no place in responsible reporting.

* Be balanced in reporting about situations of war or conflict. For example, when reporting about the Palestinian-Israeli conflict, provide the same quality and depth of coverage you give to suicide bombings in Israel, to Israeli house demolitions, arbitrary arrests, beatings and killings of Palestinians. Include human-interest stories and photographs of Palestinians living under occupation.

* Seek the opinions of Muslim experts. Muslims should define themselves in the discourse relating to Islam just as experts from other religions and ethnic groups are consulted on issues relating to that group. As the fastest growing religion in America, and the largest minority group in the United States, Muslims should also

be included in religious perspectives on contemporary issues.

* Cover non-crisis events in the Muslim world, e.g. international Islamic conferences, Muslim achievements and contributions, and other human-interest stories.

* Regularly cover human-interest stories or events relating to American Muslims, such as holidays, community events, Muslim achievements, and local and national conferences

* Irresponsible media coverage that plays on fear and hate is immoral and unjust and can itself result in prejudice and violence against innocent people, especially women and children. Hysterical fear and hatred have caused injustice and harm to numerous groups in our history including Native-Americans, African-Americans, Germans, Japanese, and those accused of communist tendencies during the McCarthy era. Today, American Muslims find themselves victims of discrimination in schools, college campuses and in the workplace, and regularly experience anti-Muslim hate incidences, including threats, harassment, stereotyping, property damage and physical assaults.

APPENDIX E :
Useful contacts, further information
Key Muslim Organizations in the US

American Muslims for Global Peace & Justice
Santa Clara, CA: (408) 988-1011 www.global-peace.org

The Council on American-Islamic Relations (CAIR)
Washington, DC (202) 488-8787 www.cair-net.org

Council on Islamic Education (CIE)
Fountain Valley, CA (714)-839-2929 Email: info@cie.org

Islamic Circle of North America (ICNA)
Jamaica, NY (718) 658-1199
www.icna.org

Islamic Society of North America (ISNA)
Plainfield, IN (317) 839-8157
www.isna.net

Islamic Networks Group (ING)
San Jose, CA (408) 296-7312www.ing.org

Muslim American Society (MAS)
Falls Church, VA (703) 998-6525 mas@masnet.org
Chicago, IL (877) 222-1083 ImamW.D. Muhammad

Good Reference Books and Videos
General books on Islam
The Essential Quran by Thomas Cleary
The Bible the Qur'an and Science by Maurice Bucaille
Islam and Media coverage

Silent No More: Confronting America's False Images of Islam by Paul Findley
Covering Islam by Edward Said

Inspiration

Rumi a Spiritual Treasury by Juliet Mabey
Gems of Wisdom Heart of Gold: Inspiration from the past for

people of the future by Javed Muhammad

Convert and Revert stories

Daughters of Another Path: Experiences of American Women Choosing Islam by Carol Anderson Anway, Carol L. Anway

The Autobiography of Malcolm X by Alex Haley

Audio and Videos

Audio speeches by Hamza Yusuf, Dr. Hakim Quick and Anwar Al-Awlaki

Islamic songs by Yusuf Islam, Dawud Wharnsby Ali and Zain Bhikha

Book of Signs video based on the book "The Bible, The Quran and Science"

Muhammad: Legacy of a Prophet (PBS)
2 hour documentary about Prophet Muhammad and Islam in America

The Message: Film on the life of the Prophet Muhammad

Useful Web Sites

Great Overall sites on Islam:
www.islamicity.com
www.discoverislam.com
www.beliefnet.com
www.islam101.com
Great sites for Non-Muslims and comparative religion.:
www.thetruereligion.org
www.beconvinced.com
www.themodernreligion.com
Islamic News:
www.iviews.com
Work related issues:
www.workpositive.com
E-commerce (Books, videos, audio-tapes):
www.astrolabepictures.com
www.soundvision.com

A Profile of US Muslims

Demographics
• 50% earn more than $50,000 annually.
• 58% are college graduates.
• 69% are married.
• 36% were born in the US; the rest come from 80 other countries
• 32% are South Asian, 26% Arab, 20% African-American, 7% African, and 14% are 'other.'
• One-fifth are converts to Islam.

Politics:
• 79% are registered to vote.
• 40% are Democrats, 23% Republicans, and 28% Independents.
• 36% are moderate, 27% are liberal, and 21% are conservative.
• They are liberal on some issues - 93% favor both universal healthcare and more generous government assistance to the poor -and conservative on many social issues: They support the death penalty (68%); oppose physician-assisted suicide (61%); support a ban on pornography (65%); and favor making abortions harder to obtain (57%).
• They support prayer (53%) and the display of the Ten Commandments in schools (59%), and favor vouchers for private schools (68%).

Participation in American Life:
• They support donations to non-Muslim social service programs (96%); getting more involved in civic organizations (96%); and participation in the political process (93%).
• They take part in groups helping the poor, sick, elderly, or homeless (77%).
• They take part in school or youth programs (69%).

Impact of Sept. 11:
• 58% approve President Bush's handling of terrorist attacks.
• 66% agree the war is being fought against terrorism, not Islam.
• 68% say the military effort could lead to a more unstable Middle East.

• 51% support military action.

• 67% say a change in US Middle East policy is the best way to wage war against terrorism.

• 61% say the US should reduce its support of undemocratic regimes in the Muslim world.

The poll was supported by Project MAPS: Muslims in the American Public Square, a project of the Pew Charitable Trusts.

Glossary

A

Adam: The first human being and Prophet

Adab: Manners, etiquette

Ahl al-kitab: "People of the Book," refers to Jews and Christians who received the previous revelations

Akhirah: The next life (here-after)

Allah: Arabic word for the One and only True God, Creator and Sustainer of all creation

Allahu Akbar: God is most Great

Alhamdulilah: All Praise is due to God, phrase used by Muslims to thank Allah

As-salaamu alaykum: Islamic greeting meaning peace be upon you

Ayah: "a sign," a verse from the Quran

Ayatullah: Major religious leader of the Shiites

B

Bismillah: "I begin in the name of Allah" invocation said at starting any good activity.

C

Colonialism: Time period between 17th to 20th centuries when Europeans occupied and ruled most of Africa and Asia. A large part of these lands belonged to Muslims.

Crusades: A series of Christian Holy wars which targeted the Muslim lands including Jerusalem. Started in 1099 until 1270 when under leadership of Salahuddin (Sala Din) Jerusalem was recaptured by the Muslims and wars brought to an end.

D

Dawa: Invitation to Islam

Din: "way of life" which is a broader definition than "Religion"

Duaa: Supplication (prayer), calling upon God

E

Eid al-Fitr: The celebration marking the end of the month of Fasting, Ramadan. Fitr is a charity given so that all Muslims can celebrate this day.

Eid al-Adha: The celebration marking the conclusion of the Pilgrimage, Hajj. A lamb or other animal is sacrificed and shared with family, neighbors, and the poor.

F

Fatwa: A legal ruling or opinion given by a qualified Islamic scholar

Fitrah: The inner "moral compass" of guidance given by God to all human beings at birth

G

Gibreel (Gabriel): The angel who brought the revelations to the Prophets including the Quran to the Prophet Muhammad (PBUH)

H

Hadith: "Tradition," sayings of the Prophet Muhammad which have been recorded. The two most famous and authentic ones are by Bukhari and Muslim

Hajj: Pilgrimage to Mecca, 5th pillar of Islam and compulsory on all adult Muslims who are able to go

Halal: Permissible

Haram: Unlawful, Prohibited

Hikmah: Wisdom

Hijab: refers to covering and/or head scarf worn by Muslim women

Hijrah: Start of the Muslim calendar marking emigration of the Prophet Muhammad in 622.

I

Imam: "Leader" of the prayer or for the community

Iman: Faith or belief

Insha Allah: God willing, used to refer to all future events
Isa: Arabic name of Jesus
Islam: Submission to Allah, Peace, and the name given to the faith of Muslims

J

Jihad: Striving in the cause of Allah
Jannah: Paradise
Jerusalem: Third holiest city which includes the Masjid Al-Aqsa and the Dome of the Rock where Prophet Muhammad ascended on the journey to the heavens (Miraj)
Jumah: "Gathering" refers to the Friday noon congregational prayers

K

Kabah: Cube shaped building in Mecca, which is the first house of worship built for mankind
Kafir: "One who hides or covers the truth". Reference to non-believers
Khalifah: Caliph (leader of the Muslim nation)
Khutba: Sermon delivered on Fridays or Eid prayers

L

La ilaha illa Allah Muhammad ar Rasoolulah: "There is no God but Allah and Muhammad is His Messenger." The declaration of Muslim faith (Shahadah)

M

Madarsa: School where Islamic subjects are taught including memorization of Quran
Mariam: Arabic name of Virgin Mary
Masjid: A place of prostration, a mosque
Mecca: Holy city of Islam in present Saudi Arabia. Muslims turn towards the Holy Mosque and the Kabah inside at time of prayer
Medina: "The city" where Prophet Muhammad emigrated to, established the first state, and was buried. Second holiest city

after Mecca

Muhammad: The last in the chain of Messengers from Adam through Abraham, Moses, and Jesus (Peace Be Upon Them all)

Mujahidin: One who does Jihad

Muslim: One who submits to and obeys the laws of God

N

Nabi: A Prophet

Niyyah: Intention

Nation of Islam: Blended various teachings into an organization founded by Elijah Muhammad in the 1930s in the US. Malcolm X, and, later, Elijah Muhammad's son Imam W.D. Muhammad denounced his fathers teachings after his death, and most African Americans followed.

O

Ottoman Empire: The last Muslim Caliphate brought by the Ottoman Turks which stretched from the Balkans to the Middle East (1453-1918). Dissolved by the European Colonial powers after World War II.

P

PBUH: Peace Be Upon Him, said after the name of Prophets

Q

Qibla: The direction of Mecca

Quran: Holy book revealed to Prophet Muhammad. Source of guidance for Muslims. Preserved, memorized, and unchanged since revelation

R

RA: Radiya Allah Anhu, may Allah accept his actions, said after names of the Righteous

Rahman: The "most Merciful" a name and attribute of Allah

Ramadan: Month of fasting and pillar of Islam

Rizq: Sustenance

S

Sabr: Patience and perseverance in adversity

Sadaqah: Charity

Sahabah: Companions of the Prophet

SWAT: Subhana WatAllah, used after the name of Allah

SAW: Salla Allahi wa Salaam, may Allah's peace and blessings be upon the Prophet

Salaat, Salah: Prayer and pillar of Islam. There are five obligatory prayers per day

Sawm, Siyam: Refers to fasting. Muslims fast in the month of Ramadan from sunrise to sunset for the whole month

Shahadah: Bearing witness there is no God but Allah (SWAT) and Muhammad (SAW) is his Messenger

Shia: The 2nd major branch of Islam, which split with the mainstream Sunni Islam. Shias believe the successors in leadership should come from the family of the Prophet Muhammad through Ali. Most Shias live in Iran and Southern Iraq

Shura: Mutual consultation

Shariah: The moral and legal code of Islam

Shirk: Associating others in worship with God (the only Sin which won't be forgiven) according to the Quran

Sunnah: Path or example set by the Prophet Muhammad and includes what he said, what he did and what he agreed to.

Sufi: Mystics of Islam

Surah: A chapter of the Quran. The Quran has total of 114 surahs

T

Tafsir: Explanation of the Quran

Taliban: 'Students" name of the ruling party of Muslims in Afghanistan that came to power in 1996 and was routed in 2001 by the United States and it's allies

Tawhid: Belief in the oneness of Allah (SWT)

U

Ummah: Community (or nation) of believers in Islam

W

Wahhabi: Puritanical movement started by al-Wahhab in Arabia which emphasizes need to go back to Quran and Sunna

Wudu (wuzu): Ablution or ritual washing of hands, face, and feet before starting one of the five daily prayers

Z

Zakat, Zakah: Obligatory sharing of wealth with needy, a pillar of Islam

A Note to Muslims

This book is primarily directed toward people who are not of the Muslim faith. However, I hope many sections will be interesting and inspiring even for Muslims. One of the major challenges in putting a book together is not only deciding what goes in but also what does not. So as not to confuse the message I have avoided addressing Muslims throughout this book, except for this very small note.

No matter where Muslims live we have and will continue to feel the reverberations of the tragic event of September 11, 2001. The primary goal of writing this book is to reach out to people of other faiths especially in North America and Western Europe. I do not represent all Muslims and there is no way I could even attempt to express the views and opinions of Muslims, the world over.

I have been blessed to live in three lands: England, Japan, and the United States. For those of you whose only image of these countries and people is through television and other media let me say that the "average" American or British or Japanese knows very little about Islam. When things flare up in different regions of the Muslim world some of them do get visibility. September 11 has brought Islam and Muslims to the world stage. We are under scrutiny and it is up to us to demonstrate by our actions what the real Islam is. Anyone in principle can become an American and anyone in principle can become a Muslim. As an American Muslim all I have done is touch upon some of the common values that we love and uphold.

It is easy to point fingers whenever something "bad" happens to America or Israel or whoever. However, we as Muslims need to take a look in the mirror and reflect on what the Quran and our beloved Prophet(PBUH) have taught us. How did we get into this predicament and more importantly how do we get out? There are no easy answers, no easy demons to quash. Our struggle is not between Islam and America; it is ultimately between those who embrace certain human values and those that do not, between the haq (righteousness) and the batil (wrong).

Our issues are rights, not just Muslim rights but human rights. However, if we want the world to lend us an ear, sympathy for just causes, we have to get our own house in order. We cannot allow mixed messages to permeate from us to those who in the first place know very little about Islam, or to those few who will take any opportunity to show us in poor light. As Muslims we need to take personal responsibility. We cannot expect that somebody else is going to take care of our troubles and the reality as we know is that Allah does not change the condition of a people until they change themselves.

Take a look in the mirror. What do you see?

May Allah grant not only Muslims but all humanity His guidance and light, His peace and His justice.

Assalamualikum.

Permissions
1. Peace: The Greater Jihad by kind permission of Yahya

2. FAQs on 9-11 Attacks Regarding Islam and Muslims by kind permission of Islamic Networks Group (ING)

References

Unless otherwise specified information was obtained in public domain off the web.

1. There was once a civilization by Carly Fiorina, CEO Hewlett Packard (Speech given on Sept 26, 2001)

2. Historical Perspective by Syed Abul Ala Maududi

3. Enemies, Hercules and what they said about Muhammad: from Tabari, Volume 2, Page 651.

4. Basics of Islam: adapted from several sources including Discover Islam. The purpose of life: Reference www.usc.edu/dept/MSA/

5. Economic and Political System of Life: Islam by Ghulam Sarwar

6. My body is my own business by Naheed Mustafa

7. The veiled (hijab clad) woman: a poem

8. Post Colonial Fever: Content referenced and adapted from The Gala Peace Atlas by Dr. Frank Barnaby

9. President George W. Bush on Islam: Remarks at Islamic Center of Washington, D.C., 2001

10. A Storied Glorious Religion: by Rabbi Marc Gellman & Msgr Thomas Hartman, Newsday, 1/26/2002

11. America's Enemy (original title "Islam is not America's Enemy" by Claire Britton-Warren)

12. My American Jihad by Zayed Yasin

13. Muslims against Terrorism (various).

14. Quotes by Muhammad Ali on 9-11 (various sources)

15. Islam is Here (poem by Jawad Ahmed)

16. Love & peace Messages, courtesy of the Muslim Community Association, Santa Clara, CA

17. Building Bridges Between Islam and the West by Prince Charles: From the Prince's speech, December 15, 1996

18. A Christian and Muslim Prayer: from Muslim Primer by Ira Zepp

19. The Church and Islam: M. Abbot, The Documents of Vatican 11, London 1967, p. 663).

20. The Ten Commandments By Shaid Athar, MD

21. Parallel Sayings of Muhammad and Buddha: www.convert-stoislam.org
22. Empathy Poem: Amy Maddox from Teaching Tolerance
23. Islamic Stories of the past, inspiration for the future by Hamza Yusuf Hanson from Forgotten Roots
24. Story about Mansur Ibn Mihran and servant from "Good neighbors and other moral stories." By A. Busool
25. Justice for all: Adapted from Islam and World Peace by M.R.Bawa Muhaiyaddeen
26.The Pleasantries of the Incredible Mulla Nasrudin by Idries Shah
27. Rumi a Spiritual Journey from the Sufis: from Rumi a Spiritual Treasury by Juliet Mabey
28. Gary Miller Reference: www.themodernreligion.com Muslim converts: their stories
29. America land of plenty, land of poverty: what Islam has to offer the world: Ref "Islamic Solutions" by Hamza Yusuf, Islamic Horizons April 1994, On Being Human by Erich Fromm
30. Appendix A: Timeline of important events in Islamic history
31. Appendix B: Muslim World Population source: "The World Factbook 2001", CIA and www.geohive.com/global/world.php
32. Appendix C: Guidelines regarding accommodating Muslim practices Islamic Protocol, Guidelines for Employers, Schools, Neighbors from Islamic Society of North America (ISNA) and Council on American Islamic Relation (CAIR)
33. Guidelines for the media on reporting about Islam or Muslims by Islamic Networks Group (ING)
34. A Profile of US Muslims: Conducted in November 2001 by Zogby International
35. We Believe in His Books from "Islam, Our Choice": Extracted from The Muslim's Belief by Shaikh Muhammad as-Saleh Al-'Uthaimin. Translated by Dr. Maneh Al-Johani
36. Sections, Prophethood of Muhammad, Polygamy, Status of Jesus adapted from "Top misconception about Islam" By Huma Ahmad

INDEX